BETWEEN ROOTS AND WINGS

CRAFTING MY PATH

NANDKUMAR KHAIRNAR

To my father, **Rajaram Khairnar,**

Your unwavering support has been my foundation,
and your wisdom, my guiding light.

You have taught me the beauty of staying rooted in tradition
while giving me the courage to spread my wings and soar.

This book is a tribute to the balance you embody—
honoring where we come from while embracing the dreams ahead.

With deepest love and gratitude,
Nandkumar

Contents

Foreword

A Journey of Growth and Discovery

"Between Roots and Wings" is not just a book; it's a story about finding the right balance between where we come from and where we want to go. We all face this challenge: how do we hold onto our past while still reaching for our dreams?

This book discusses this struggle and shows that real change often occurs when we learn to let go and hold on.

Through insightful stories and personal experiences, the book invites us to explore the journey of growth. It's like a mirror, reflecting our lives and a guide, helping us find our way.

The wisdom in this book will stay with you at every stage of your life. It encourages you to think deeply about yourself and how you can grow.

As you read, take some time to think. What keeps you grounded? Where do you see yourself going? Whether you are looking for direction, healing, or simply a better understanding of yourself, "Between Roots and Wings" will guide you. Let it inspire you to honor your past and embrace the future, finding the right balance between both.

Dr. Hemant Ostwal

Director, Suyash Hospital, Nashik

Motivational Speaker

Author of "Pankh Sakaratmakteche" (Wings of Positivity).

Preface

Have you ever felt torn between two worlds? One part of you longs to stay connected to your past—your family, your traditions, and the place where you grew up. These are your roots, strong and deep, giving you a sense of belonging.

At the same time, another part of you dreams of exploring new possibilities, taking risks, and discovering what lies beyond the familiar. These are your wings, urging you to soar and embrace the unknown.

Between Roots and Wings is a story about finding harmony between these two powerful forces. It explores how our past shapes us while reminding us of the importance of growth, change, and forging our own path.

This book encourages us to cherish our roots while also having the courage to spread our wings. It is a celebration of tradition and transformation, proving that we don't have to choose between where we come from and where we want to go—we can embrace both.

I hope this story inspires you to honour your past while reaching for your dreams.

Nandkumar Khairnar

Prologue

The scent of freshly carved wood filled the air as Arun ran his fingers over the intricate patterns on the wooden panel. His father, Ravji, stood beside him, carefully guiding his chisel with steady hands. Each stroke was precise, every curve a reflection of generations of craftsmanship passed down through their family.

"Pay attention, Arun," Ravji said gently. "This craft is not just about carving wood. It is about preserving our heritage, our identity."

Arun nodded, but his heart was restless. He admired his father's mastery, yet something inside him longed for more. His eyes drifted to the small sketchbook hidden under his workbench—filled with designs unlike anything ever created in their workshop. Bold, modern, different. He wanted to show them to his father, but fear held him back.

As the evening sun cast long shadows across the workshop, Arun watched his father at work. Ravji's hands moved with practiced ease, shaping the wood into patterns that had been unchanged for generations. For a moment, Arun wondered—was this the only path he was meant to follow?

The distant hum of the village, the rhythmic sound of chisels against wood, and the weight of his family's legacy surrounded him. Yet in the quiet corners of his heart, another rhythm called—a whisper of new possibilities, a longing to carve his own path.

Between the roots that held him firm and the wings that urged him to fly, Arun stood at the edge of a decision that would change everything.

CHAPTER ONE

Whispers of Change

A warm golden light spilled over the treetops, catching on dewy leaves that shimmered in their glow. Thin trails of smoke rose lazily from rooftops, the familiar scent of burning cow dung mingling with the rich, earthy aroma of the land. Soft streaks of white and pink brushed the horizon, while a gentle breeze whispered through the village, carrying the faint chirping of birds. The town and the land stirred together, quietly greeting the peaceful beauty of the morning.

The narrow paths between homes were still damp from the night's rain, releasing a sweet, earthy fragrance. Thatched roofs, dark with moisture, glistened under the soft light of dawn as smoke from kitchen fires warmed the cool air. As the villagers started their day, their footsteps left light footprints in the ground, each step fitting into a familiar rhythm.

Children, their faces bright with energy, chattered excitedly as they prepared for school, their cheerful laughter spilling into the streets. Mothers hurried them along, handing them tiffins and adjusting school bags, while the elders, seated on their verandas, watched with knowing smiles. The school bell rang out in the distance, a signal of routine yet full of promise, as young feet hurried along the paths. The children's carefree laughter contrasted sharply with the elders' measured, deliberate pace. The elders' faces, lined with age, reflected a lifetime of wisdom and experience. The town hummed with its daily rhythm, held together by the unspoken understanding between generations. The warm, nurturing atmosphere created by the combined efforts of extended families was the heart of the community. Nestled amidst this scene of life stood Ravji's workshop—a weathered but sturdy building, the stone walls smoothed by decades of use, standing proudly as a symbol of the village's enduring craftsmanship. The town, usually a vibrant tapestry of sounds and scents, now settled into an evening hush, each nuance a reminder of the deep-rooted traditions that bound them together.

The fields glowed green against the misty backdrop, and the forest gently rustled in the breeze.

Inside Ravji's workshop, the scent of sandalwood filled the air, mixing with the tang of freshly cut timber. The room was bathed in a soft, filtered light that danced across the worn floor, creating playful shadows. To one side, a large, scarred workbench stood, its surface marked by years of careful work.

The tools, each meticulously arranged, lined the walls or rested on the bench: carving knives with sharp, curved blades for rough shaping, gouges with curved edges for deep cuts, and chisels with flat blades for precision work. The mallet, a sturdy companion for striking tools, was always within reach. Nearby, a bench hook held the wood securely, and detail knives for intricate designs rested in their designated spots. V tools and U-tools, essential for creating specific grooves and hollows, completed the array. It was a haven of painstaking creation, where each item had its proper place and every tool had its intended use, rather than merely a workspace.

The workshop hummed with the steady rhythm of craftsmanship. Ravji worked with quiet confidence, his hands guided by years of experience, as he shaped a wooden panel into a delicate floral pattern. Each deliberate stroke of the mallet showcased his unwavering dedication to the craft. The air, heavy with the scent of sandalwood, created an atmosphere that was both invigorating and intense, a blend of comfort and focus.

Within this haven of order and tradition, Ravji dedicated himself to embodying the craftsmanship of generations past. The workshop stood as a living tribute to woodcarving's enduring legacy.

A soft chorus of clinking cups and saucers mingled with their easy conversation and laughter. Wisps of steam curled into the air, blending with the earthy scent of wood shavings that lingered from the morning's work.

The conversation drifted between village gossip and the upcoming festival. Even as they spoke, Ravji's hands remained steady, his focus unwavering on the delicate piece of wood. Watching him work, his friends were awestruck by his precise movements, honed by years of practice. They realised this was more than a craft; it was a living tradition that connected them to their ancestors.

"Ravji, that piece has been keeping you busy for ages," Dashrath commented, leaning against the wooden bench. His eyes sparkled with curiosity. "What's the latest project?"

Ravji, still focused on his carving, paused to sip his tea. "A design for the festival. I thought I'd try something different this time."

Bhagirath, a man with a wide grin and a tilted white cap, chimed in as he stirred his tea. "I'm sure it'll be great! Everyone in the village was talking about last year's decorations, you know. No pressure, but I think everyone's expecting even bigger and better this time!"

Ravji chuckled softly, glancing up from his work. "Glad to hear that. Despite our best efforts, finishing it on time is always a challenge. You know how it is."

Vitthal, a burly man with a thick mustache, stroked his cheek thoughtfully. "With all the farm work piling up, it's a miracle we get any festival prep done. But somehow, we always manage."

Dashrath took a slow sip, nodding in agreement. "Especially with the new well coming in. Might give us a bit more time to help with the decorations this year."

Bhagirath leaned in, his grin widening. "Let's just hope they don't delay it. Last year, everything was so rushed, my wife nearly pulled her hair out trying to get all the sweets ready."

The group laughed; the sound was warm and light, blending with the workshop's soft rhythm. Ravji smiled, his eyes crinkling at the corners. "We always find a way, don't we? Tradition keeps us going."

As the conversation shifted between village gossip and the upcoming festival, Dashrath glanced at the sun climbing higher in the sky. "Well, Ravji, we should let you get back to your work before the sun takes the whole day," he said with a knowing smile.

Bhagirath stood, brushing the dust from his dhoti. "True. Our tasks are waiting for us. But good tea as always, Ravji."

Vitthal extended his arms upwards, loosening his muscles and finding relief. "Best of luck with the new design," he added, nodding towards the bench.

The men bid farewell, their voices growing distant as they vanished down the winding paths. Ravji returned to his workbench, his hands instinctively grasping the carving knife. The workshop was filled with the rhythmic sounds of creation. Before striking the chisel, he paused to examine the wood, his fingers tracing its grain. A steady, purposeful tap set his careful shaping of the wood in motion.

Arun emerged at the workshop door, the small square windows letting in the soft light of the day. His father, Ravji, was already at work, his hands moving delicately as he carved a familiar floral pattern into the wooden panel on his workbench. The scent of fresh-cut timber filled the air, mingling with the faint aroma of sandalwood that always seemed to linger in the space.

"You're up early," Ravji remarked, not looking up from his work.

Arun smiled faintly, stepping inside and running his fingers along the worn surface of the workbench. "Couldn't sleep. Thought I'd get a head start."

Ravji nodded, still focused on the delicate curve he was etched into the wood. "Good. There's plenty to be done today." He gestured toward a stack of unfinished panels near the back of the workshop. "Those need smoothing, and the borders could use some fine detailing before we varnish."

Arun looked at the pile—the work routine, but not new. He picked up one of the panels, running his hand over its rough edges. "I'll get started on those then."

They worked in companionable silence, the steady rhythm of tools against wood filling the space. Arun's movements were precise and deliberate as he smoothed the rough edges. His mind, however, was elsewhere. He occasionally observed his father, noting the ease and accuracy with which Ravji carved elaborate designs.

"You've got a good hand for detail," Ravji commented, observing Arun's work. "That attention to detail will be essential for the temple panels next week. They've asked for something special, and we'd prefer traditional floral patterns. People like what's familiar."

Arun nodded, though something stirred in him. "Yeah, traditional is... reliable."

Ravji chuckled softly. "Reliable has been our lifeline all these years. Never underestimate its value, Arun."

Arun smiled, but inside, his thoughts raced. He respected tradition, of course, and admired his father's mastery of it. But a part of him craved something else. Something different. He glanced around the workshop, his eyes settling on the tools laid out meticulously, each with its purpose. His bold, modern designs lay untouched on the side table, a testament to his hesitation to share them.

"I was thinking," Arun started slowly, keeping his tone light, "what if we tried something a little different for the smaller commissions? You know, just as an experiment."

Ravji paused briefly, considering his son's words. "Different how?" His voice was open, inviting Arun to elaborate

"Maybe sharper lines, abstract forms. People are seeking something unique these days. For larger orders, we could stick with tradition, but for smaller pieces, we could try something different," Arun suggested, observing his father's expression.

Ravji didn't answer immediately. He finished the curve he was working on, setting his tools down carefully. "Arun, people come to us because they're assured of getting what they want. Tradition is steady and dependable. It's like an old song—people hear it and feel connected. I'm not saying no to new ideas, but... there's a balance.

Don't lose sight of what got us here."

"I understand," Arun said, his voice quiet. "But what if there's a way to bring both together? To keep the soul of what we do but give it a new form?"

Ravji smiled slightly, wiping his hands on a rag. "Maybe there is. But for now, let's focus on what's in front of us. The orders won't finish themselves."

Arun nodded, picking up his tools again. The conversation drifted back to routine matters—the upcoming projects, the temple orders, and the repairs needed for the workshop roof. Their familiarity and shared experiences provided a grounding presence as they worked side by side.

Yet, as the hours passed, Arun's thoughts were magnetically drawn to the unfinished piece in the corner of the workshop. It had been there for years—a project his father had started but never completed. Every time he looked at it, he felt a strange pull—a desire to finish what had been left undone, but in a way that was distinctly his own. Despite his deep respect for his father, he longed to carve his path.

Could he do it? Could he complete the piece his way without betraying the legacy his father had built?

Arun's hand faltered, the chisel slipping slightly against the wood. He took a deep breath, steadying himself. He wasn't sure if he was ready to take that step yet. But the idea lingered, a quiet tension within him that he couldn't shake.

For now, his focus remained on the present task. But the decision to follow his father's path loomed on the horizon.

As the evening sky deepened from amber to a dusky purple, Ravji's house glowed warmly with the soft flicker of an oil lamp. The day's work was done, and the family gathered in their small living room, the air heavy with the comforting scent of Vatsala's cooking. A simple clay stove still radiated warmth in the corner, and the faint crackle of burning wood created a gentle backdrop to the sounds of the evening.

Vatsala, her sari neatly around her, served chapati and vegetable curry on brass plates. "Arun, have some more," she urged, offering him another piece of bread. Her motherly instinct always ensured no one left the dinner hungry.

A soft smile played on Arun's lips as he shook his head from his cross-legged position on the floor. "I'm full, Aai. The curry is perfect, as always.

Ravji, seated beside him, brushed the dust from his hands, his face marked by the fatigue of a long day. He looked at Arun with a quiet sense of satisfaction. His eyes sparkled with unspoken pride. "How did the work go today? Everything running smoothly?"

Arun nodded, but a slight hesitation lingered in his expression. "Yes, Appa, it was productive. I completed the carving for the door frame today. But..." His voice trailed off as if contemplating his next words.

Vatsala glanced between them, sensing a deeper conversation but not pressing the matter. "It's fantastic that you're learning. Your father's artistry is in your blood."

Ravji's eyes softened in response. He turned to Arun, his tone more relaxed, as if it were a regular part of their evening routine. "The festival's coming up soon. I'll need your help with the final touches. We've got a lot to finish."

Arun smiled faintly, though something in his gaze seemed distant. "Of course, Appa. I'll be there."

Vatsala, sensing the underlying tension, changed the topic with a bright smile. "The women in the village were talking today. Everyone is eager to see the new designs, Ravji. Especially the temple decorations. They think this year's will be even grander than the last."

Ravji chuckled softly, leaning back against the wall. "We'll see about that. Plenty of work to do before anyone can call it grand."

He paused, glancing at Vatsala before continuing. "I'll be gone for a few days next week. The temple committee from the nearby town has asked for my help with their festival preparations. It's a big order—woodwork for their altar and pillars. They're looking for someone skilled in the field, and they've asked me to lead the project.

Vatsala raised her eyebrow in surprise. "A whole week? That's a long time, Ravji."

He nodded. "Yes, it is. But it's for the festival, and I couldn't say no. I'll leave early Monday morning and should be back by the weekend. Arun will have to manage the workshop while I'm gone."

Vatsala looked thoughtful, then smiled. "It'll be better for Arun. He'll get a chance to handle things, to show you what he's capable of."

Ravji sighed, his face etched with concern. "I just hope he's ready. There's a lot at stake, and I don't want any mistakes while I'm away."

Vatsala placed a comforting hand on his shoulder. "Trust him, Ravji. He's your son. He'll rise to the challenge."

The conversation meandered between village news, weather, festival preparations, and other small, unremarkable events of daily life. Arun just listened, a quiet sense of relief settling over him as the conversation flowed. His mind drifted in and out of the talk, yet a newfound lightness kept anchored him in the comfort of knowing a week of space to pursue his ideas without his father's watchful eye.

The stars sparkled through the open window. Inside, the warmth of the room and the gentle rhythm of the family's routine offered a fleeting moment of peace, a small respite before the next day.

Ravji stretched and sighed, his joints protesting with a soft creak as he rose. "Arun, lock up the workshop for the night. I may go to sleep now." Arun nodded and prepared to leave for the workshop. "

Arun nodded, following his father's instructions and stepping out into the cool night air. Vatsala watched them go; her heart warmed by the familiar scene, even as she sensed the undercurrents stirring within her son. She gathered the plates, her mind already turning to the next day, yet mindful of the quiet shifts happening under the surface of their daily lives.

The town, illuminated by a soft, silvery glow, seemed to shimmer under the gentle embrace of the moon. The thatched roofs and mud walls, formerly rustic and sturdy, now seemed delicate, bathed in the ethereal light. Their shapes were softly traced against the velvety night sky, while the trees and fields, blanketed in a quiet sheen, stood like ancient guardians, their forms softened by the moon's caress. The tranquil town seemed caught between two eras, rooted in tradition yet hinting at an unwritten future. Arun took a deep breath, the weight of his ancestors' legacy pressing down on him. A silent expectation urged him to continue his ancestors' legacy.

In the town square, people whispered as they gathered. They were laughing and telling stories that made everyone feel connected. The children were already asleep, dreaming about playing.

But Arun's mind was restless. The moonlight crept into the workshop, slipping through the narrow windows and casting sharp, uneven shadows on the walls, where his father's meticulous carvings stood as silent witness to generations of craft. Now still, they contrasted sharply with the movement of Arun's hands, a reminder of the ongoing legacy. Yet in the corner, a flickering flame from a small oil lamp revealed Arun, hunched over a wooden block, his hands moving with a blend of certainty and doubt. His fingers gripped the chisel with a hint of hesitation, each movement deliberate yet uncertain.

The workshop felt alive with the presence of generations past, a silent reverence lingering in the air. Arun's eyes rested on the old tools, their wooden handles worn smooth by the touch of his ancestors. Each tool seemed to carry the weight of tradition, a time when every stroke had to be perfect, where precision reigned and creativity was bound by the fear of failure. The worn tools of the past contrasted sharply with the clean, new ones beside them. Bathed in moonlight, these new tools hinted at bolder possibilities, challenging Arun to forge his path.

Arun's heart raced as he worked, the chisel slipping slightly in his hand. His breath caught. Was this a mistake, a sign that he was straying too far from what he knew? He steadied himself, pushing the doubt aside. This was Arun's time—his chance to bring his ideas to life without the constant scrutiny of his father. He knew Ravji would never approve of what he was doing. The design he was crafting defied everything he had been taught. It was bold, asymmetrical, and deliberately imperfect—a stark departure from the flawless symmetry that defined his father's work.

In the dim silence of the workshop, Arun's hands paused over the wood, but his mind raced faster than the tools could move. The silence in the room was palpable, filled with the weight of unspoken expectations. His father's shadow loomed over the old tools, their worn handles almost sighing under the burden of duty and tradition. They sat in their places, heavy with years of careful craftsmanship, each one a reminder of the precision his father demanded. The new materials gleamed under the flickering light, tempting Arun with their untapped potential. They seemed to pulse with the thrill of something daring, different—promising a path that had never been taken. His fingers twitched, caught between reaching for the comfort of the past and the lure of the unknown. Every stroke and pause was a step on the path he was carving for himself, both in the wood and his future.

As Arun's fingers followed the jagged, uneven lines of the carving, the travelling merchant's words echoed in his memory: "Not like anything we've seen around here, is it? These pieces arrived from cities far beyond the horizon. Artists there aren't afraid to break tradition." The man's eyes twinkled with mischief as he spoke.

Flipping through the pages, Arun was captured by the bold, abstract shapes and vibrant colours—so different from the intricate, precise designs his father valued. He had murmured to himself, "It's strange but beautiful."

His voice lowered to a hushed tone. "Art isn't just about what others think, lad. It's about what you want to say. Sometimes, you have to carve your path."

Those words lingered in Arun's mind, igniting a deep... deep desire to break free from the village's rigid traditions. The images haunted him, fuelling a yearning to create something unique. He was certain the town would frown upon his departure from the norm, but in that instant, nothing held more weight than the fire burning within him. He felt truly alive for the first time, carving not just wood but a part of himself.

Arun vividly recalled himself as a child, barely tall enough to see over the bench. His father, Ravji, stood beside him, guiding his small hands over the smooth surface of a wooden block. The pride in Ravji's eyes was unmistakable as Arun carved his first simple design, a delicate flower. "Excellent work, my son," Ravji acknowledged proudly. Arun had beamed with pride, feeling as though he was following in the footsteps of a giant.

But as the years passed, Arun's excitement to create his designs grew, only to be met with subtle dismissals. He remembered one evening in particular when he had shyly shown his father a sketch—a bold, asymmetrical design was unlike anything in their workshop. Ravji had glanced at it, his expression unreadable, before quietly setting it aside. "Focus on mastering the basics first," he had said, his tone firm but not unkind. Arun had nodded, hiding his disappointment, but the memory of that moment lingered in his heart.

Standing within the familiar walls of the workshop, those memories returned with bittersweet clarity, bringing with them the image of his father's pride but mixed with an unspoken desire for him to continue the tradition without deviation.

Arun sighed, the conflict within him deepening. The memories of his father's pride were precious, but they also carried the weight of tradition that had shaped his life. Breaking away seemed a betrayal, not just of his father's teachings but of their father-son relationship. He knew that if he didn't break free, he would remain trapped, a mere echo of his father, his voice forever muted.

These flashbacks and reflective moments brought a wave of melancholy, underscoring the difficulty of his decision. Arun was torn between the comfort of his father's legacy and his yearning for his identity. Stepping out of his father's shadow and into the light would be difficult, requiring him to leave behind the safety of tradition.

The workshop's silence was shattered by a creak as the door opened, hesitantly, as if reluctant to disturb the sacred space. His breath hitched in his throat. plunging the corner into darkness. The workshop felt different now, the shadows looming larger, more menacing as if the walls were judging his every move.

"Who's there?" a gruff voice asked. Arun recognized it immediately. It was Damodar, the senior carpenter, who had worked alongside his father for years. Arun held his breath, his senses alert, as the footsteps drew closer. The faint light from the moon illuminated Damodar's figure as he approached.

"What are you doing here, Arun?" Damodar's voice was stern, tinged with concern. He squinted in the darkness, his eyes catching the unfinished carving on the workbench, and exclaimed, "What is this?"

Arun hesitated, his mind racing for an excuse, but he knew it was futile. Damodar had seen enough.

"It's just... an idea," Arun replied, his voice betraying the tension in his chest. He could feel Damodar's gaze on him, heavy with unspoken disapproval yet tinged with something else—understanding, perhaps?

"An idea?" Damodar repeated, his voice questioning, stepping closer to inspect the carving. His fingers hovered over the jagged lines, tracing them with a slow, deliberate motion. The silence between them was thick with unsaid words. Arun noticed the older man's hesitation, the tension between tradition and the desire to safeguard this young man from his ambitions. Finally, Damodar spoke, his voice soft, almost reluctant, as if he knew the implications of what he was about to say. "This isn't the way we do things, Arun. "Your father... he won't be happy to see this."

"I'm not trying to disrespect him," Arun said quickly, though he could feel the heat rising in his cheeks. "I just wanted to try something different."

"Different?" Damodar shook his head slowly. "We've been following the same traditions for generations."This—" he gestured to the carving—"is... unusual."

He had spent countless nights dreaming of this moment, of creating something truly his own. He would not let it go.

"I understand," Arun said, though his voice lacked conviction. "But I need to do this, Kaka. I need to see where it takes me."

As Damodar's eyes softened, Arun thought he saw a fleeting flicker of regret. "Just be careful, Arun said quietly, his voice carrying the pain of choices not made and paths not taken. "The path you're taking... it's a risky one. Don't wander too far, or you might experience being lost, as I did."

Arun's heart sank at the older man's words, the gravity of the warning settling in. Damodar's voice had carried the weight of experience, the sorrow of lost opportunities, and the pain of unfulfilled potential. A wave of uncertainty washed over Arun. He didn't know if he was forging a new path or wandering. Would this lead to a glorious future, or would it be a path that led nowhere?

As Damodar's footsteps faded in silence, Arun exhaled; he didn't realize he had been holding. The workshop was silent again, but the tension in the air was palpable. Arun knew the risks, but he was determined to continue. The seed of rebellion had been planted, and there was no turning back.

Alone in the darkness, Arun's hand hovered over the tools, trembling with uncertainty. His father's legacy, once a source of pride, now felt like a heavy chain. But as he gripped the carving knife and began to carve again, he felt something shift within him—a quiet resolve, a determination to find his way, even if it meant stumbling along the path. As the knife bit into the wood, the old and the new collided in a dance of creation and destruction, forging a legacy uniquely his.

A sense of purpose radiated from Ravji as he entered his workshop that morning, his usual quiet demeanor replaced by an infectious enthusiasm. News of a major and demanding project from a nearby town had arrived the day before—a project that would keep him occupied for months. His eyes sparkled with purpose, and his usually quiet demeanor was lighter, lifted by the excitement of challenging work.

"Big job, this one," he had told Vatsala the previous night with a smile. "The temple in Shirur needs carvings for their new prayer hall. It'll be demanding but rewarding work.

As he stepped into the workshop, the comforting scent of freshly carved wood and varnish filled his lungs. He stopped briefly, taking in the familiar arrangement of his neatly placed tools. The room was bathed in soft light, casting long shadows over the workbench that bore the scars of countless past projects. Every tool, worn smooth from years of dedicated use, seemed to hum with life, waiting for his skilled hands to bring the next creation.

As he reached for a block of teakwood, his eyes caught sight of something unusual. In the far corner of the workshop, partially hidden beneath a cloth, was a piece of wood that didn't belong. His heart raced as he walked over, a sense of unease settling in his chest. He walked over and pulled back the covering. What lay before him stole the air from his lungs, leaving him momentarily frozen.

The carving was unlike anything he had ever seen—jagged edges, uneven patterns, and a design that defied the traditional symmetry he held so dear. It was chaotic, almost rebellious in its form, as if it were daring to challenge the very foundation of his craft. Ravji was momentarily speechless, struggling to grasp the sight before him. Ravji's fingers trembled as he traced the unconventional lines, his breath uneven. A raw energy, a spark of creativity in the carving unsettled him. He felt a pang of fear as if it were a warning of something unknown, but he quickly dismissed the thought. This wasn't the time for doubt

Who could have done this? The truth slammed into him: Arun was the only one with after-hours access to the workshop. The thought filled him with a mix of disbelief and disappointment. How could the boy he had nurtured and mentored deviate so far from the laid-down path?

Just then, Arun stepped inside a slight smile on his face. The smile vanished as soon as he spotted his father standing beside his work, Ravji's face a blend of shock and disappointment.

"Appa," Arun began, his voice tentative, "I was going to tell you about this."

Ravji turned to face him, his eyes narrowing. "What is this, Arun?" he asked, his tone sharp. "What have you done?"

Arun took a steady breath. He had anticipated this moment. 'It's a new direction I'm exploring,' he stated firmly. 'A blend of our traditional methods with modern design.

Ravji's silence was heavy, his gaze like a physical weight on Arun. When he finally spoke, his words carried the sting of disbelief and a deeper sense of betrayal. "This isn't different, Arun. This is a mockery of everything our family has stood for. Have you forgotten the values and traditions I've taught you?"

"Of course not!" Arun's words tumbled out faster than he intended. "I respect everything you've taught me, but I also believe that we need to evolve. The world outside our town is changing, and if we don't adapt, we'll be left behind."

Ravji shook his head, his face hardening as he struggled to suppress the growing turmoil. Arun's words struck a deep resonance within him, bringing to the surface a fear he had long tried to suppress. But he couldn't allow himself to acknowledge that now. "Our craft isn't meant to change with the whims of the outside world. It's meant to preserve our heritage and our identity. You talk of evolution, but all I see is destruction."

Disappointment washed over Arun. He had poured his heart into every imperfect line, only to be met with this. How could his father not recognize this?

"It's not destruction, Appa," Arun argued, his voice growing louder. "It's evolution. It's about taking what we know and making it relevant for today. "Don't you see? If we keep doing the same thing, we'll become obsolete. Our work will lose its meaning."

Ravji's eyes flashed with anger. But beneath the anger was something deeper—a fear that Arun's words might be true, that the traditions he had spent his life preserving might one day fade into obscurity. "And who are you to decide what has meaning?" He shot back. "You're still a boy, Arun. You haven't earned that experience to understand the importance of tradition. You think you're so clever with your modern ideas, but you're forgetting the responsibility that comes with this craft. It's not just about you—it's about our family, our ancestors, and the legacy they left us."

The words stung, but Arun refused to back down. "I am aware of the responsibility of that legacy," he said, his voice trembling with emotion. "But I also know that honoring your legacy means building upon it, not simply replicating it."I have to find my path, even if it means taking risks. I'm not trying to disrespect our heritage, Appa; I'm trying to breathe new life into our heritage, ensuring its continuation for generations to come."

Silence filled the workshop, the air thick with tension. Ravji stared at his son, his face unreadable. In his father's eyes, Arun saw a battle between the desire to uphold tradition and the reluctant acknowledgment that change might be inevitable. Yet the walls Ravji had built around himself and his beliefs were unyielding. Too strong. Arun held his breath, anticipation mingling with apprehension as he waited for his father's response.

But when Ravji finally spoke, his voice was cold and final. "You will stop this foolishness immediately," he commanded. "You will not go on with this... this abomination." As long as you are in my workshop, you will follow my rules, and you will respect the traditions that have been passed down to you. Do I make myself clear?"

Arun felt his heart sink. He had expected resistance, but the harshness of his father's words cut deeper than he anticipated. He felt cut off, like a door had slammed shut. He knew that working on this project would mean defying his father, risking everything he had worked for. Yet the thought of abandoning his vision and giving up on what he believed in was unbearable.

"Yes, Appa," Arun whispered, his voice barely audible. But as he said the words, he knew they were a lie. He could never abandon his dream—not now, not after coming this far.

Ravji gave a curt nod, as if the matter were settled, and turned back to his workbench, leaving Arun frozen in place, fists clenched. The older man's movements were precise and deliberate—the picture of calm compared to Arun's inner turmoil. Brewing inside Arun. But even as Ravji resumed his work, a shadow of doubt lingered in his mind, a tiny seed planted by Arun's words, growing in the darkness of his thoughts.

Arun performed his tasks mechanically all day, but his mind was elsewhere. The confrontation with his father had only solidified his resolve.

He couldn't—wouldn't—abandon his project. His father might not understand now, but one day, Arun was certain he would see the value in what he was trying to do.

Later that evening, the faint glow of the oil lamp filled the modest kitchen. Arun sat silently on a low stool. His hands played absentmindedly with the fingers, his thoughts heavy with the confrontation that had unfolded earlier. His mother, Vatsala, moved gracefully around the small space, the familiar sounds of her preparing the evening meal soothing but unable to reach the storm inside Arun.

Vatsala, always attuned to the subtle shifts in her son's appearance, noticed the tension in his face and the heaviness in his silence. She set the ladle down and approached him, her voice soft and concerned. "Arun, what's troubling you, Beta? You've been so quiet since you came home."

Arun glanced up at her, the weight of the day pressing hard on his chest. He hesitated for a moment before finally speaking. "It's Appa. We argued."

Vatsala frowned, kneeling beside him with her hand resting on his arm. "What happened? Tell me."

With a deep sigh, Arun began to recount the conversation. "He called my work foolishness, Aai. He doesn't understand why I want to do something different, something that's never been done. He doesn't see the value in it. He told me to stop. But... I can't. "I've poured so much of myself into this, and walking away now would feel like leaving a piece of my soul behind."

Vatsala's brow furrowed, her heart aching for her son. She could hear the hurt and frustration in his voice, and it hurt her to know that the two people she loved most in the world were at odds. "Arun, your father... He's a man of tradition. It's not that he doesn't care about you or your ideas; it's just that he's always known one way of doing things. Change frightens him."

The frustration simmering within him finally boiled over, and Arun shook his head. "But why can't he see, Aai? Why can't he understand that we need to move forward? This craft is about more than just repeating the same patterns."

Vatsala took his hands in hers, her touch warm and reassuring. "I know, beta. I know how much this means to you. And I understand that you want to honor the craft in your way. But your father—he's spent his whole life perfecting the work passed down to him. His tradition is fundamental to his very being."

Arun's eyes glistened in the low light, the weight of his emotions heavy. "What am I supposed to do, Aai? If I follow Appa's path, I lose myself. I must find my way. But if I go against him, I'll lose him too."

Vatsala's heart broke a little at his words, her fingers wiping away the tear that threatened to fall from his eye. "Listen to me, Arun," she said softly, her voice full of maternal wisdom. "You don't have to choose between the two. There's always a way. I'll talk to your father. I'll find a calm moment to speak with him and help him see your perspective. He loves you, even if he finds it difficult to express that right now.

Arun looked into his mother's eyes, searching for hope. "You think he'll listen to you?"

Vatsala smiled gently, her gaze steady and filled with affection. "He always listens to me. "I'll show him that your dream isn't an abomination, but a different perspective to honor the craft. "We'll find a middle ground, beta. But you have to be patient. Let me talk to him when the time is right."

Arun nodded, the tension in his shoulders easing slightly. "Thank you, Aai. I don't know what I'd do without you."

Vatsala patted his hand and stood up, returning to her cooking with quiet grace. "You'll never have to find out. We're in this together, Arun. Just give it a little time."

As the evening wore on, the warmth of her words lingered in the air, soothing the unrest that had taken root in Arun's heart. He sat there longer, watching his mother move about the kitchen, the soft clinks of the pots and pans like a lullaby. He was uncertain about the future, but his mother's presence offered comfort, making it feel less daunting.

The weight of the previous evening's argument settled heavily upon Arun as he awoke. The weight of their argument lingered in his mind, a constant reminder of the rift between them. Seeking solace, he turned to the temple, where he had always found peace.

Arun walked through the town, mirroring the doubts that clouded his thoughts. The temple stood at the town's edge, its ancient stone walls illuminated by the golden light of dawn. Arun entered quietly, his footsteps echoing softly in the space. He kneeled before the idol, his mind a swirl of emotions.

"Am I wrong?" he whispered, his voice barely audible. With stress in their minds, he sat in a corner with closed eyes, praying to God and wishing for the blessings of God and his parents.

As Arun stepped into the courtyard, he spotted Fakira sitting under the shade of the old neem tree, gently strumming his worn-out sitar. Fakira, the elderly craftsman, was a close friend of his grandfather. Arun smiled and gave a slight bow while greeting. "Namaste, Baba," he said as he made his way over. Fakira's wise and kind eyes seemed to peer into Arun's troubled soul; he stopped playing and looked up with warm, knowing eyes.

"Arun," he called softly, his voice carrying the tenderness of someone who had seen much in life. "You carry a heavy weight today, my boy. What's on your mind?"

Arun hesitated for a moment, then let out a quiet sigh. Sitting beside the old man, he opened up about the conflict swirling inside him—the struggle between honoring his father's expectations and following his path.

Fakira listened with patient silence, nodding thoughtfully as Arun's words tumbled out. After a big pause, the elder spoke, his voice gentle but firm. "You remind me of a verse from the Gita," he said, his eyes reflecting the wisdom of the ages. "It is better to perform one's duty imperfectly than to perform another's perfectly." Fakira's words hung heavy in the air, each syllable echoing in Arun's mind. Fakira's voice softened. "Your path may be challenging and etched with flaws, Arun, but it is uniquely yours. Only by walking will you discover your true self."

A quiet certainty began to settle in Arun's mind, like the first clear ray of sunlight breaking through a fog. He thanked Fakira and returned home with renewed resolve, ready to embrace his journey, imperfections and all.

That night, long after Ravji had retired to bed, Arun returned to the workshop. The room was bathed in moonlight, silent and still. He approached the corner where his unfinished work lay and picked up his tools. The familiar smells now mingled with the tension deep within Arun's chest. The carving was rough, its lines uneven, reflecting the struggle between tradition and innovation that played out with each stroke of the chisel. Yet, with each stroke, a soothing calm settled over Arun as he carved the wood and his destiny.

In the stillness of the night, with only the moon as his witness, Arun made a silent vow—to continue his work, to find a way to honor his father's legacy while forging his path. This was his rebellion, proving that tradition could evolve without being destroyed. This was his rebellion, his way of honoring both the past and the possibilities of the present. And as the night stretched on,

Arun's resolve hardened. He would continue his work, no matter the cost. This was only the beginning.

CHAPTER TWO

Carving Uncertainty

Arun sat at the edge of his workbench, the dim light from the workshop's solitary bulb casting long shadows across the room. The intricate carving he had been working on was almost complete—a blend of traditional patterns with modern, asymmetrical lines. His fingers hesitated over the wood, trembling slightly as he carefully placed the piece on the table. The room was silent, save for the soft rustling of leaves outside, and the quiet seemed to amplify the doubts swirling in his mind.

"Do you think it's worth doing?" The question hung in the air, barely audible, as he spoke.

A quiet footstep echoed from the doorway. Bharat had been standing there, leaning casually against the frame, watching with the same patient curiosity that had marked their friendship for years. He stepped forward, the wooden planks creaking under his weight, and took in the piece on the table. His gaze moved slowly as if absorbing the weight of each stroke and each intention behind the design. His eyes, always sharp and discerning, moved over the curves and lines with the practiced ease of someone who understood the work intimately, even if he couldn't replicate it himself.

Silently, Bharat traced the edges of the design with his fingers, his touch gentle but deliberate. The carving's texture, rough where Arun had let emotion guide his hand, told a story of struggle and resilience. His gaze conveyed admiration, but it also revealed an appreciation for the effort behind this creation. The silence between them, laden with unspoken support, was their language—a quiet acknowledgment of battles fought and still to come.

"Arun," Bharat said firmly, his voice intense. "This isn't just a piece of furniture—it's you. Bold, unique, everything you've been striving for."

Arun frowned, biting his lip as he considered Bharat's words. The weight of his father's expectations pressed down on him, heavy and suffocating. "But what if my father sees this? He's been so clear about sticking to tradition. What if this isn't just risky but downright wrong?"

Bharat let out a low, thoughtful hum. He glanced at the carving and Arun, again, his expression softening. "Your father's legacy is important, but so is your voice. This piece merges the old with the new—it's not about dismissing tradition but about expanding it. Think of it as honoring the past while paving your path."

Arun's eyes flicked back to the carving, the doubt still evident in his gaze. He traced a jagged line with his thumb, feeling the conflict embedded in the wood. The design was a leap from the traditional carvings his father, Ravji, taught him. The path ahead felt uncertain, a precarious balance between honoring the past and forging his own future. "I hope you're right," he murmured, his voice tinged with uncertainty.

A playful glint entered Bharat's eyes as he smiled, a familiar expression Arun always found reassuring. However, beneath the playfulness, a flicker of something else emerged—a rare vulnerability that Bharat typically concealed. "Sometimes, that tightrope leads to the most rewarding places, Arun. You've already done something remarkable by daring to blend the tradition with the new idea. That's what makes your work stand out. "This will be a challenging journey, and that will shape you. Challenging generations of tradition requires more than courage; it demands a willingness to risk everything. But the rewards will be worth the struggle."

Arun's mind drifted to his childhood—memories coming in fragments, sharp and vivid. He recalled the hours spent watching his father carve intricate designs with precision and care, the pride in Ravji's eyes as he passed down the knowledge of their craft. But alongside those memories were moments of frustration—the countless times Ravji had dismissed Arun's ideas as too radical, too different.

"Arun, you've always been different," Bharat said, pulling him gently back from his thoughts. "And that's not a flawed thing. Your father's work is incredible, but so is yours. You're not trying to replace him—you're trying to add to the legacy."

Arun nodded, drawing strength from the memory of his conversations with Bharat about his designs. Bharat had always understood his desire to innovate, to bring something new to the craft that had defined his family for generations. He had been the one to motivate Arun to embrace this risk and display his work at the art fair, despite the possible repercussions.

"Do you remember when we sneaked into the city and saw that modern art exhibition?" Bharat asked, a wistful smile spreading across his face. "That's when I knew you. were destined for something different. You were mesmerized by the sculptures, the way they broke the rules and still created something beautiful."

Arun laughed softly at the memory. "Those pieces so inspired me. They were like nothing I'd ever seen, and I wanted to bring that same sense of wonder into my work."

"Bharat's eyes locked onto Arun's with unwavering intensity. "And you certainly have." His voice resonated with conviction, each word emphasizing the truth of his statement. However, a flicker of uncertainty crossed his eyes—a rare acknowledgment of the stakes involved. "This piece—it's meant to blend the old and the new, and you've done it brilliantly. Yes, it's risky. But the greatest rewards often come from taking chances. You've already achieved something remarkable."

Arun's eyes softened with gratitude. "You've always believed in me, even when I doubted myself. I don't know what I'd do without you, Bharat."

Bharat shrugged, a knowing smile playing on his lips, but the sincerity in his gaze deepened, revealing a flicker of his vulnerability. "You'd probably still be hiding in this workshop, afraid to show the world what you're capable of. It's okay to be scared, Arun. I am too, sometimes. But that's when you know you're doing something that matters."

The two friends sat in silence, the gravity of the decision hanging between them. Bharat had always been more than just a companion; he was the one who saw Arun's potential long before Arun himself did. Their bond had been forged in countless moments—a shared laugh over a botched project, late-night talks about dreams too big for their small town, and silent support when words failed.

Arun sighed, his shoulders relaxing slightly. "Thanks, Bharat. Those were the words I needed to hear."

Bharat chuckled a gentle rumble that brought a twinkle to his eyes. With a playful nod toward the door, he beckoned Arun to follow, a lightness in his demeanor that invited camaraderie. "Well, then, let's get this show on the road. "The art fair is waiting, and so is the world. Go out there and show them what you can do!"

"Speaking of the art fair..." Bharat's eyes twinkled as he leaned closer, his voice dropping into a secretive tone. "I just heard some breaking news—you won't believe it. "Guess what? There's an art fair next week.". All sorts of artists will be there—painters, sculptors, craftsmen like you, showing off their work."

Arun's heart skipped a beat. "Next week? Are you serious?" His voice wavered between excitement and disbelief.

Bharat nodded, grinning. "And guess what? It's the perfect chance for you to showcase your work. No Appa watching over your shoulder, no restrictions—just you, your art, and a real opportunity to make your mark."

A surge of excitement coursed through Arun. With Ravji about to leave, this could be his chance. Excitement battled with apprehension within Arun.

"This... this could be it, Bharat." Arun's voice trembled, excitement and anxiety dancing in his eyes. He glanced at the floor, then back up, his heart racing. "I could finally present my work, my way. Away from Appa's watchful gaze, free from all the traditions I'm expected to uphold." The words spilled from him, each one heavy with the promise of what could be.

Bharat's expression softened, and he placed a reassuring hand on Arun's shoulder, the warmth of his touch grounding him in the moment. "You've always had it in you, Arun. The art fair is just the beginning. It's time to show the world what you've been holding back."

A surge of emotion filled Arun's chest—excitement, fear, and the undeniable thrill of a new beginning. "You think I can do this?"

Bharat smiled, his eyes sparkling with encouragement. "I know you can." And remember, this isn't about replacing your father's legacy. It's about adding to it. You have to be brave enough to let the world see it." "You have the talent; all left is to be brave enough to share it."

Arun nodded, a slow smile creeping onto his face. Arun felt a surge of anticipation at the thought of the art fair and the freedom Ravji's absence would bring. "I'll do it, Bharat. This is my time."

Bharat's grin widened, and he clapped Arun on the back. "That's the spirit! This is your chance to carve your path. And when your father sees what you're capable of, I'm sure he'll understand."

As the two friends exchanged a moment of quiet understanding, the gravity of Arun's decision enveloped him. For the first time, a flicker of hope ignited within him—that maybe, just maybe, he could finally emerge from his father's shadow and craft something that was truly his own.

This was more than just an art fair—it was the beginning of his journey, his opportunity to take a risk and prove to himself that his ideas were worth pursuing.

Stepping into the morning light, Arun's heart thrummed with anticipation. The familiar town now held uncharted promise. The road ahead was his to define, and with Bharat at his side, he felt a surge of confidence. The art fair was his first step, and he was ready. Today, he would not follow—he would carve.

Days turned into hours as the art fair approached, his anxiety growing. His workshop, once resonant with the steady rhythm of his father's work, now pulsed with fresh energy. He poured himself into his work, each stroke a delicate dance between honoring his family's tradition and forging his bold style.

The piece resting beneath his hands was unlike anything his father, Ravji, would have ever created. It was a wooden wall hanging, bold and intricate, but with a flair for the unexpected. Instead of the familiar geometric patterns and delicate florals Ravji was known for, Arun's design blossomed into spirals—abstract shapes that grew and twisted outward from the center, defying the rigid symmetry of their traditional roots. Arun envisioned it as a metaphor for his life—his heritage at its core, yet stretching and evolving into something uniquely his own.

Vatsala, with her intuitive understanding of his moods, often visited the workshop during the peaceful afternoons, anchoring him amidst the chaos of his thoughts. She would sweep the shavings from the floor and sit on a small stool in the corner, watching Arun work without interrupting. There was a comforting quality to her silent companionship, marked by her subtle gestures of support.

One evening, as the golden light of dawn spilled through the windows, she approached him. I'm so proud of how hard you've been working, beta," she said softly, placing a gentle hand on his shoulder. Your father may not see it yet, but I do. What you're creating is your creation, and don't let anyone make you think otherwise."

Arun paused, her gaze meeting his, and for a fleeting moment, his anxieties subsided. "I'm not sure if it will be received well, Aai," he admitted softly, setting down his tools, "but your unwavering support gives me the courage to pursue it." "It's different. It's not what they expect."

Vatsala gave him a small, knowing smile. "Being different is not a flaw. Sometimes, people need time to see what's in front of them.

And sometimes, it's not the eyes that need convincing, but the heart."

Her words echoed in Arun's mind as he returned to his work. Though Vatsala had never been vocal in challenging Ravji's stern adherence to tradition, her quiet encouragement had always been his secret source of strength.

Over the next few days, Arun poured his energy into a series of new creations, infused with his modern approach. His next creation was a set of small, finely carved bowls. At first glance, they seemed traditional, with floral motifs etched delicately around the rims. But inside each bowl, Arun had carved angular shapes that gave the impression of something breaking from within. He envisioned it as a representation of his journey—holding onto tradition while allowing space for innovation.

Bharat, Arun's closest friend, became a familiar presence in the workshop, his energy lighting up the space. Each day, he burst through the door with an eager grin, his eyes sparkling as he examined Arun's latest creations. He leaned in closer, his hands gesturing animatedly as he shared his thoughts, the passion in his voice infusing each moment with electricity.

"You're onto something, Arun," Bharat said one morning, leaning over the table to admire the wall hangings Arun had just finished. "These will stand out for sure."

"I hope so," Arun muttered, though his hands moved with less confidence than Bharat's words suggested. His mind kept circling back to the same worries. What if people didn't understand his work? What if the elders, so used to Ravji's designs, saw Arun's innovations as a step too far?

"Don't doubt yourself," Bharat added, sensing his friend's hesitation. "People will remember what's different, not what's the same. You've taken the best of what we know and made it your own. That's what they'll see."

Arun nodded, but the storm of doubt inside him refused to quiet. Despite his nod, the weight of his family's legacy and his father's expectations continued to haunt him.

Thoughts raced through his mind, keeping him awake. He pictured his work displayed at the art fair for all to see. He envisioned the villagers, their eyes filled with doubt and disdain. Worst of all, he imagined his father's eyes, full of disappointment at what he might see as a rejection of the traditions Ravji had spent his life upholding.

But Arun was driven by something deeper than fear—an untamable fire that refused to let him turn back. He had poured too much of himself into these pieces to stop now. They weren't just wood and designs; they were his heart, his identity, his defiant declaration: "This is me."

One afternoon, as Arun stood at his workbench, refining the edges of the final bowl, Vatsala entered the room with a basket of freshly made chapatis. The aroma of the warm, soft bread filled the air, but she lingered by the doorway, watching her son. Arun glanced up and met her eyes, and for a moment, neither spoke. The silence between them was comfortable yet heavy with unspoken emotions.

Vatsala moved closer, placing the basket on a nearby table with a gentle thud. Her eyes, warm and knowing, met Arun's. "Your father loves you, Arun," she said softly, her voice carrying a depth of understanding. She paused, eyes hovering over him, the unspoken words flickering in her glance. "His love may not always be visible, but it runs deep, unwavering, and true. The path you're carving for yourself—it's not a departure from him. There's space in your journey for both your vision and his."

Arun swallowed hard, her words heavy in the air. "I don't want to hurt him, Aai." But this—this is who I am. I don't know if he'll ever accept that."

Vatsala reached up and gently cupped his cheek. "Sometimes, love isn't about agreeing on everything. It's about understanding, even when we see the world differently. Your father's path was never meant to be yours, Arun. You've carved your own. And he will see that, in time."

Her words lingered as his eyes swept over the scattered pieces, his fingers tracing their edges, each a part of his story. But the familiar tug of perfection gnawed at him. Would the elders see what he saw? Could they understand that tradition had to evolve to survive?

The day before the art fair, Arun began packing his creations carefully. He placed the wall hangings in a cloth-lined crate, his hands lingering over the spirals that swirled across the wood. The bowls, too, were wrapped with care, their designs sharp and unconventional but undeniably his own. His heart raced as he surveyed his work, a mixture of pride and doubt swirling within him. He had done all he could. The rest was up to fate—and the people who would soon judge his creations.

The final piece, Arun's masterpiece, was a bold departure from tradition. This large, intricately carved wooden sculpture defied gravity and his father's legacy, embodying a new beginning.

"The Unfurling" was inspired by the lotus, a flower deeply rooted in Indian culture and spirituality, symbolizing purity, growth, and rebirth. But this was not a traditional depiction. Arun had reimagined it entirely. The sculpture's foundation was grounded in the familiar, with delicate, symmetrical petals carved in his father's perfected style. But as the eye traveled upward, the petals began to break away from their structured form, twisting and unfurling in bold, flowing arcs that seemed to burst from the core, as if the flower was coming alive, stretching toward something new and unseen.

The work was dynamic, almost chaotic, yet each line and curve revealed the careful thought and craftsmanship behind it. The polished, warm wood reflected the light, casting shadows that gave the petals a sense of movement.

Arun had spent countless hours perfecting this piece. It had been his most ambitious project, a true reflection of his journey. The lower part represented his roots—his respect for tradition and the foundation his father had built. But as the sculpture rose, it became something entirely different: a testament to Arun's vision and his belief that tradition could evolve and expand without being lost. The flowing lines, unbound and free, were a symbol of his yearning for creative freedom.

As he worked on "The Unfurling," Arun's thoughts often drifted to his father. He knew this piece would stir strong reactions at the art fair. Some might see it as a bold new direction for their craft, while others—especially Ravji—might view it as a challenge to tradition. And yet, Arun couldn't bring himself to alter it. This was his statement, his truth, and no matter how much he wrestled with the doubt that gnawed at him, he couldn't silence the voice that urged him forward.

Vatsala sat beside him during the long days of preparation, her hand resting gently on his shoulder. She could see the worry etched on his face, the weight of uncertainty pressing down on him. Her steady touch reassured him, a silent testament to her unwavering belief in his abilities and her deep concern for his well-being. "You've created something beautiful, Arun," she said, her voice filled with warmth. "I can see the care and love in every detail."

Arun sighed, running a hand through his hair. "I'm worried no one will see it the way I do. Especially Baba.

Vatsala smiled softly, her eyes reflecting both wisdom and love. "Your father is set in his ways, but that doesn't mean he won't recognize the passion behind your work." Tradition is important to him, but so is your journey of self-discovery. He may not say it, but he wants you to be proud of your work—just as he is of his."

Arun looked at her, her words resonating deeply. It was rare for his mother to speak so openly about Ravji and even for her to offer such direct encouragement. Her quiet strength had always comforted him, but tonight, her words offered something new: hope.

"Thank you, Aai," he murmured, feeling the tension in his chest ease just a little.

With a gentle smile and a squeeze of his shoulder, Vatsala said, "Whatever happens at the fair, Arun, you've created something beautiful. Don't forget that."

With her words echoing in his mind, Arun finished the final touches on "The Unfurling." The next morning, he carefully wrapped the sculpture and packed it onto the cart with the rest of his creations. Looking at the crates that held so much of his heart, a familiar unease crept over Arun. The excitement of the fair, the thrill of showing his work, was overshadowed by one lingering fear.

What would Ravji make of this?

A knot of uncertainty tightened in his chest, but resolute determination also stirred within him. The fair wasn't just about his craftsmanship but was about revealing his true self. Whether the town embraced or rejected his work, Arun had carved his path with his own hands.

As he took the reins of the cart, with Bharat beside him, Arun felt the weight of the day ahead. His feet were firmly planted on the road to the art fair, but his heart was still tethered to the unknown. Outwardly, his hands were steady on the reins; inwardly, he trembled at the thought of his father's reaction.

He was ready. But whether Ravji was ready still loomed large, casting a long shadow over the path ahead.

The art fair was a kaleidoscope of colors and sounds. Stalls stretched across the open grounds, each alive with the vibrant works of artisans across the region. The air thrummed with excitement—lively conversations, the gentle clink of handcrafted goods being inspected, and bursts of laughter dancing on the breeze. Above, the sky was a brilliant canvas of blue, and the sun bathed the fair in a warm glow that made every hue pop with intensity. The scent of freshly carved wood, varnish, and incense mingled in the air, creating an intoxicating aroma that felt like the very spirit of the craft on display.

His booth, nestled between two larger, more traditional setups, felt like an outsider. On his right, a stall showcased meticulously painted idols, each figure capturing divine beauty with deep-rooted skill. To his left, intricate wood carvings displayed elaborate designs that followed generations-old patterns, every detail flawlessly executed. Arun's display, in contrast, was a bold departure from the norm—an attempt to merge tradition with modernity, featuring asymmetrical lines and unconventional forms that challenged the established standards.

Arun's hands trembled faintly as he arranged his pieces, each one a fusion of traditional craftsmanship and contemporary design. The significance of the occasion pressed against him, a quiet but insistent force. This wasn't merely an art fair—it was a test, a moment to discover whether his bold ideas could find footing in a world that often resisted change. His pulse quickened, a storm of anticipation and unease churning within him as he prepared to greet the fair's first attendees.

As he stepped back to admire his display, the sun stretched shadows across the ground, its light skimming the edges of his carvings, giving them an almost ethereal shimmer. Yet, beneath this serene surface, turmoil churned inside him. Arun's thoughts raced to the endless nights he'd spent in solitude, the gouge in his hand biting into the wood with each deliberate stroke—a silent defiance against the expectations that had always loomed over him. His father's voice, firm, seemed to reverberate in his mind, carrying with it the weight of generations—a legacy he both revered and resisted.

The image of Ravji's stern face loomed large in his mind. He could almost hear his father's disapproval, his voice echoing with the weight of generations of tradition. But alongside that, another voice—Bharat's—kept reminding him that this was his opportunity to step out of the shadows.

"Arun," a familiar voice called out, breaking his thoughts.

Bharat's arrival lifted the heaviness that often settled over Arun's mind, bringing with it a lightness that felt both rare and welcome. Dressed in a simple but neat kurta, Bharat moved with a confident stride, his eyes sparkling with his characteristic enthusiasm. Arun and Bharat had shared a bond since their earliest days, and Arun had always been struck by his friend's ability to confront life's hurdles with a rare blend of resilience and wit; his laughter was never far away. Today, however, there was a new seriousness in Bharat's demeanor—a seriousness that hadn't been there before, as if he too understood the weight of this moment.

"Looks like you've got everything set up," Bharat said, clapping Arun on the back.

"Yeah," Arun replied, though his voice lacked confidence. "But I'm not sure if anyone will get it."

Bharat's gaze traveled across the booth, lingering on the carvings that stood apart, their uniqueness a stark contrast to everything else on display. Though his smile was genuine, the faint shadow of worry in his eyes sent a ripple of unease through Arun. He had seen Bharat look like this when they were younger, standing at the riverfront, daring each other to jump into the unknown waters below. Bharat had hesitated at the river's edge, just as he now seemed to pause as if recalling his own time facing the unknown.

"Arun, you've poured your soul into these pieces." Don't worry about their comprehension; concentrate on showing the world who you truly are. This is your chance to shine."

Arun let out a sigh, his gaze drifting back to his work. The dread of his father's disapproval loomed large, casting a shadow over his pride. He knew Ravji's discovery would shatter the fragile peace between them. His father's voice echoed in his mind, a constant reminder of the tradition he was expected to uphold. But alongside that fear, there was a spark of something else—a flicker of hope that maybe, just maybe, he was on the right path.

"But what if Appa finds out? He'll be furious. He's always been so adamant about sticking to tradition."

Bharat's expression softened, his grin fading into something more reflective. A flicker of vulnerability crossed his eyes as if he comprehended the weight of attempting to satisfy loved ones while remaining authentic to oneself.

"He will be, but you can't let that hold you back. Think of this as a bridge between tradition and your voice. You're honoring the past while creating something innovative. But I won't lie to you, Arun—this isn't easy. You're entering a new space, and it's natural to feel afraid, but that's how you grow. But it's also necessary."

Arun nodded, but the knot in his stomach remained. His eyes scanned the fairgrounds, watching as visitors moved from stall to stall, admiring the work of artisans who had mastered the craft in ways that Arun could only dream of. The traditional stalls seemed to draw the most attention with their flawless designs and familiar forms. Arun felt like a stranger, as though he didn't belong, his creations standing out awkwardly amidst the flawless craftsmanship surrounding him.

"I hope you're right. This piece—it's meant to blend the old and the new, but I'm worried it's too risky."

Bharat's grin widened, though his eyes remained serious. "That's exactly it! The biggest breakthroughs happen when you dare to step into the unknown." And remember, I've been where you are now. I've taken that leap. No matter what happens, you've already achieved something amazing by daring to be different."

Arun's heart was swelling with gratitude for his friend's unwavering support, but the doubt lingered. He wanted to believe that this was the beginning of something that could bridge the divide between the world he came from and the world he aspired to explore. But the fear of failing—of letting his father down—loomed large, casting a shadow over the fragile hope he was trying to hold onto.

The fair continued in full swing, with visitors moving from stall to stall, admiring the artistry on display. Arun couldn't help but feel pride as a few people stopped at his booth, their eyes lingering on his work. The sight of strangers pausing to admire his carvings sent a thrill through him—a small but significant victory in a day filled with uncertainties. For the first time, Arun began to feel that maybe his work had a place in this world, that there were people out there who could see the value in what he was trying to achieve.

A small spark of hope started to grow inside him, but it was quickly met with a chill as he noticed the familiar figure.

Damodar, the senior carpenter from Arun's town, stood at the edge of the booth, his face twisted in a disapproving frown. He glanced over Arun's pieces, his lips curling into a sneer. The stark contrast between the traditional work surrounding him and the bold, asymmetrical designs in Arun's booth seemed to fuel his disdain.

"What is this, Arun?" Damodar demanded sternly, his voice laced with disdain. "These are not the techniques Ravji taught you. This... this is an insult to our craft."

Arun's heart pounded in his chest, the confidence he had felt just moments ago crumbling under Damodar's harsh gaze. The carving, once a bold declaration, now seemed to crumble under Damodar's gaze, as if on the verge of collapse. The words of encouragement from Bharat began to fade, replaced by the familiar weight of fear and self-doubt.

Before Arun could respond, another voice cut through the tension—calm yet commanding.

"Is this your work?" a woman's voice, soft but firm, asked, drawing both Arun and Damodar's attention.

Arun turned to see a well-dressed woman standing beside his booth, her eyes keenly focused on the display. She was older, with a dignified presence that exuded authority and warmth. Her silver-streaked hair was tied back in a neat bun, and she wore a simple yet elegant saree that spoke of understated sophistication.

"Yes, ma'am," Arun mumbled, his words faltering as her unexpected appearance left him flustered. "It's my work."

"I am Saarika Desai," she introduced herself, her voice calm but with an air of quiet authority. A well-known curator with a discerning eye for craftsmanship, she nodded thoughtfully, stepping closer to examine one of the pieces. Her eyes, sharp and discerning, moved over the carving with a mixture of curiosity and appreciation. Her gaze held a depth that suggested she wasn't merely viewing the surface—she was peering beneath, comprehending the narrative woven into each chisel stroke.

"Interesting. Very interesting," she murmured, her voice contemplative. "What inspired you to create something like this?"

Arun hesitated, his eyes flicking between Damodar and Saarika. "I... tried to blend the traditional techniques I learned from my father with modern elements I've come across in books and other works."

Saarika smiled a hint of amusement in her approving gaze. "You've captured something truly unique. Your work creates a dialogue between past and present—a conversation between generations. You respect tradition, yet you boldly push its boundaries. That's a remarkable quality."

Damodar, glaring at the carving, scoffed loudly, his voice dripping with scorn. "Conversation? This is nothing but a mockery of our tradition. Arun has strayed too far from the path laid out for him. This is not the work of a true craftsman."

Saarika turned her calm, firm gaze toward him, and Damodar felt a sudden flare of anger. Her words, though measured, seemed to confront everything he had believed in and fought to preserve.

"Tradition is important, yes," she began, her voice respectful but unyielding. "But so is innovation. If we never allowed ourselves to explore beyond what we know, we'd still be stuck in the past. Tradition isn't about repeating the same patterns; it's about adapting and growing while preserving its core values.

Damodar's frown deepened as his weathered hands curled into fists at his sides. His face hardened, the lines deepening as her words ignited a silent storm within him. He knew who Saarika Desai was—a renowned curator, respected in the art world for her modern outlook and keen eye for contemporary articles. Her reputation for pushing the boundaries of tradition in the name of growth had always unsettled him.

Adapt? Grow?" His voice grew louder, edged with a mixture of frustration and fear. "If we bend our traditions, what is left to preserve? Our craft has survived because we've preserved it, not changed it on a whim."

He paused, the weight of his words hanging in the air before he continued, his tone intensifying. "You dismiss growth as easy, but you have no idea what's at stake. This isn't just about creating something new; it's about erasing our identity and everything we've fought to preserve!"

Saarika paused, her gaze shifting to the sculpture. "The Unfurling," she began, her voice softer now but full of conviction, "is a perfect example of how tradition and innovation coexist. Look at the base—those symmetrical petals, so delicately carved, are rooted in the techniques your father mastered. That part is untouched, unaltered, holding the weight of everything passed down. But as you follow the petals upward, they begin to break free, twisting and unfurling, as if the lotus is awakening. Arun isn't destroying tradition; he's allowing it to breathe, to evolve into something new while still honoring its origins."

She stepped closer to the sculpture, her fingers gently tracing the delicate contours of the petals. "In our culture, the lotus symbolizes purity and rebirth. But rebirth doesn't mean rejecting the past; it signifies growth and transformation. Arun has captured that here—he shows us that tradition doesn't have to be static. Like this lotus, it can unfurl into something dynamic, reaching toward the future while preserving the beauty of its roots."

Saarika turned back to Damodar, her expression resolute. "Change doesn't erase the past. It carries it forward. Arun's work is not a mockery of tradition—it's a tribute to it, woven with the belief that the best way to honor our heritage is to allow it to grow."

Damodar's scowl intensified, but a hint of doubt flickered in his eyes. The weight of Saarika's words hung in the air, challenging everything he thought he knew. He stood in silence, torn between the comfort of preserving the old and the trepidation of embracing the new.

His voice trembled slightly with the force of his emotions—a mix of anger and desperation. Damodar had spent his entire life upholding the traditions passed down through generations. For him, those traditions were his sacred foundation as a craftsman. The idea of change, of bending those time-honored practices to fit modern tastes, struck him as a betrayal of everything he held dear.

Looking at the artwork, Arun felt a pang of doubt. The sharp lines and unusual shapes seemed to question everything he had learned, everything he believed in. The fear of being left behind, of watching his craft become a relic of the past, gnawed at him, fuelling his resistance to what he saw as a dangerous deviation from the true path.

Saarika's expression softened, though her resolve remained unshaken. She could see the pain behind Damodar's anger—the dread of losing something precious. "I understand your concerns," she said gently, her voice carrying a note of empathy. "You've dedicated your life to this craft, and it's only natural to want to protect it. But consider this—true preservation isn't about keeping something frozen in time. It's about ensuring that it remains relevant and meaningful for future generations. Arun's work isn't a rejection of tradition; it's an evolution of it. He's finding a way to honor the past while making it speak to the present."

Damodar's breath hitched as he listened to her words, feeling a pang of doubt for the first time. He glanced at Arun, the younger man's face a mixture of hope and fear. Could it be that Arun wasn't abandoning the craft but instead trying to preserve it in his way? This thought shook him to his core, making him question everything he believed in.

The old man, however, was not prepared to give up so easily. "And what happens when the next generation comes along?" he demanded, his voice tinged with bitterness. "When will they take Arun's innovations and twist them further? Where does it end? How far do we go before we lose everything that makes our craft what it is?"

Damodar's voice trembled. He feared not just the change but the unknown that lay beyond, a future where the traditions that had defined him were lost.

Saarika met his gaze, her eyes brimming with understanding. "Change is inevitable, Damodar Ji," she said softly. "But that doesn't mean we have to lose ourselves. It's up to each generation to find the balance between honoring the past and embracing the future. Arun is trying to find that balance, which is a difficult path. But it's also necessary. If we don't allow our craft to evolve, it will wither away, be forgotten, and be irrelevant. Embracing this new growth, even if it's different, is the only way to keep our craft alive."

Damodar's shoulders sagged slightly, the fire in his eyes dimming. Damodar looked at Arun, who stood quietly, his gaze fixed on his father, vulnerability etched on his face. Damodar could see the determination in the young man's eyes—the same determination he had once felt when he was Arun's age. Something deep inside of him was pulled by the recollection of his early disobedience and the dreams he had once harbored but abandoned.

"Perhaps..." Damodar murmured, almost to himself, "Perhaps there's more than one way to preserve a legacy."

But the thought was too painful, too threatening to his sense of identity. With a final shake of his head, he turned away from the booth, his voice heavy with resignation. "But not like this, Arun. Not like this."

As Damodar walked away, his footsteps felt heavy with unspoken fears and unresolved emotions. He had hoped for his approval, but he knew that change was never easy, especially for those who had spent their lives upholding tradition. Though Damodar walked away, a small seed of hope remained, a shared love for the craft connecting them.

Observing the exchange in silence, Bharat finally spoke, his voice soft and reflective. "See? What did I tell you? You have something special here, Arun. And now, someone important has confirmed what I already knew."

Arun nodded, a small smile tugging at his lips. "Maybe you're right, Bharat. Maybe this is just the beginning."

The fair continued, Arun now standing a little taller, his confidence bolstered by the unexpected turn of events. The fear of his father's disapproval still loomed, but it no longer paralyzed him.

The words of encouragement from Bharat and Saarika echoed in his mind, mingling with the doubts that had once held him back.

Arun felt that he had finally found his place in the world today, one that he had designed out on his hands, guided by both the past and the promise of the future.

Thanks to Saarika Desai, the second day of the art fair was filled with the same excitement and energy as the first. After visiting Arun's booth, she immediately contacted Prashant Chavan, a renowned art curator and gallery owner from Mumbai, urging him to attend. She recognized that Arun's unique blend of tradition and innovation deserved a wider audience and knew Prashant was always seeking fresh talent bridging heritage and contemporary art.

By mid-morning, the art fair was bustling with activity. Arun stood behind his booth, more composed than he had been the previous day but still nervous about the reaction his work would provoke today.

"Arun!" Saarika's voice called out, pulling him from his thoughts. She approached with Prashant Chavan in tow, his tall frame and sharp attire cutting a distinct figure amidst the more traditional artisans.

Saarika smiled warmly as she stepped forward, introducing the man beside her. "Arun, I'd like you to meet Prashant Chavan," she said, her voice carrying a tone of admiration. "Prashant is one of the most respected curators in Mumbai, renowned for discovering emerging talent and seamlessly blending traditional craftsmanship with modern artistic platforms."

Prashant extended his hand, his expression thoughtful yet approachable. He stood tall, dressed in a neatly tailored blazer that hinted at his polished yet practical style. His reputation wasn't built merely on his keen eye for art but rather on his ability to connect artists with opportunities that propelled them beyond local recognition into the broader world of contemporary galleries.

Prashant's sharp, discerning eyes scrutinized Arun's pieces with the practiced gaze of a seasoned curator, yet his demeanor was warm, revealing a genuine passion for art. "You've created something special here," he said, his voice steady yet encouraging. "You've woven tradition and modern expression together, which is impressive."

"Yes, sir," Arun replied, trying to keep his voice steady. "I am attempting to honor the traditions of our craft while also exploring its potential for advancement."

Prashant's eyes narrowed as he focused on "The Unfurling." He stood silently for a moment, tracing the edges of the wooden petals with his gaze. "This is... remarkable," he finally said. "The way the traditional and the contemporary seem to coexist here, without overshadowing each other. It's rare to see such a balance."

"Thank you, sir," Arun said, his gratitude evident in his voice.

Saarika smiled, clearly pleased with Prashant's reaction, but before the conversation could continue, Fakira approached, his steady gait drawing everyone's attention.

"Ah, Fakira Kaka," Saarika greeted him warmly. "I'm glad you're here. I wanted you to meet Prashant Chavan."

Fakira nodded respectfully. "I've heard of you, Mr. Chavan. Your work in promoting our traditional arts is commendable."

Prashant returned the nod. "And I've heard of you, Fakiraji. Your influence on many of these young artisans is well known."

Just then, Sudhir Malvankar joined the group, his expression still guarded from his conversation with Arun the previous day. "So, what do we make of this modernization of our craft?" he asked, his voice laced with skepticism.

Fakira glanced at Sudhir, his expression calm but thoughtful. "Art has always been a reflection of society, Sudhir," he began. "Our traditions were once innovations themselves. The key is to find balance. To honor the past while allowing the future to unfold."

Saarika affirmed, "Exactly. Arun's work isn't discarding the old; it's ensuring our traditions resonate with future generations."

Sudhir's eyes flashed with the same deep-seated fear he had voiced earlier. "But how far do we let this go? When does tradition stop being tradition?"

Prashant, listening intently, finally spoke. "Sudhirji, I understand your concern. But tradition isn't stagnant. It's meant to evolve. The moment we refuse to adapt, we risk making it obsolete. Arun's work creates a dialogue between the past and the present. That's how we keep our heritage alive."

Sudhir's jaw tightened, the lines of his face etched with the intensity of his inner struggle. Fakira placed a reassuring hand on his shoulder. "It's difficult, I know," Fakira said softly. "But perhaps it's time to trust the next generation. They need to modernize our legacy."

Saarika chimed in; her voice was soft but firm. "Look at Arun's work, Sudhir. The base of 'The Unfurling'—that's pure traditional, untouched, and honored. But as the petals rise, they twist and reach out, like new ideas growing from the same roots. Isn't that what we've always strived for? Continuity, but with space for growth."

Sudhir sighed, his resistance softening. He glanced at Arun, who stood quietly, watching the elders debate his future. "Perhaps you're right," Sudhir murmured. "Perhaps there's room for both preservation and progress. But it's a big responsibility, Arun. Don't take it lightly."

"I won't, Kaka," Arun said earnestly. "I promise to honor the craft as I move forward."

The conversation evolved throughout the afternoon, forging a more nuanced understanding of the delicate balance between tradition and innovation. By the time the fair began to wind down, Arun experienced a renewed sense of purpose.

A father and son were admiring the carvings on display as they strolled by, the boy's tiny hand tucked into his father's, their eyes wide with curiosity. The scene before him reignited a childhood memory in Arun, pulling him into the past. He could see himself as a boy, no older than the one at the fair, standing in his father's workshop. Ravji had been patient, guiding Arun's tiny hands over the rough wood and teaching him to hold the knife just right.

Steady, Arun," his father had said, his voice firm. "Each cut requires precision. The wood will guide you if you take the time to listen."

The memory-filled Arun had a deep sense of longing. He missed those simpler days when his father's approval was all he sought. But now, standing alone at his booth, he realized how far he had come—how the path he had chosen was his own, yet deeply rooted in those early lessons.

He felt something suddenly come over him like his father was quietly watching from somewhere nearby. His heart quickened as he noticed Ravji approaching his stall, his familiar stern gaze sweeping over each piece of work. Ravji remained silent, but his disapproval was apparent in the tight line of his lips and the deep furrow of his brow. The weight of his father's unspoken judgment brought a wave of sadness over Arun, and his vision blurred as tears welled up in his eyes. Even in this moment of quiet rejection, Arun sensed the undeniable bond between them—strained but unbroken—lingering in the air between father and son.

As the sun dipped below the horizon, Arun knew that the path ahead would be filled with challenges. With guidance from mentors like Fakira, Prashant, Sudhir, and Saarika, and the wisdom of the Bhagavad Gita illuminating his path, he was ready to confront whatever lay ahead.

CHAPTER THREE

Bound by Craft, Divided by Vision

The journey back home was filled with the lingering echoes of the art fair, a mix of excitement and uncertainty swirling within him. His steps quickened with anticipation as he approached the workshop, where he noticed his father, sitting in his usual spot. A wave of surprise washed over him—Ravji had returned from his tour earlier than expected. But the surprise quickly turned to unease when Arun saw the look on his father's face, a deep-set frown that hinted at more than just exhaustion.

Ravji was acutely aware of everything—the art fair, Arun's participation—he had heard it all. Shocked and hurt, he stared at the wooden panel before him, his hands frozen. Arun felt their palpable tension as if it were a physical presence. The weight of not informing his father about the fair hung like an unspoken accusation.

"Appa," Arun began, his voice hesitant, "I was going to tell you about the fair, but..."

Ravji's response was measured and deliberate, each word like a carefully placed stone, building tension in the air. Glancing at Arun, his expression unreadable, he muttered, "You should have."

Then, thick and impenetrable silence fell between them again. It was clear this was no simple disapproval; it was something deeper. Ravji spoke only a few words, but his silence was deafening, filled with a quiet anger that threatened to erupt. Arun sensed the tension building between them, unresolved and waiting for the right opportunity to explode. With this heavy silence, they reached home.

Inside, the evening lamps were already lit, casting a warm glow across the mud walls of their home. Vatsala was sitting by the kitchen fire, her hands deftly rolling chapatis, the rhythmic clapping sound echoing through the small space. She looked up as Arun entered, her eyes softening with concern as they met him.

"How was the fair?" she asked gently, though her tone carried more than casual curiosity.

Arun hesitated, unsure how much to reveal. He didn't want to bring the tension from the fair into their home, but he also couldn't pretend that everything had gone smoothly. "It was... fine," he replied, his voice quiet.

Vatsala watched him, her brow furrowed with concern for the unspoken conflict. She glanced toward the open doorway, where Ravji had disappeared moments earlier without a word. Her heart ached at the distance growing between her husband and son, a gap that seemed to widen with each passing day.

"Appa... he didn't say much," she said cautiously, placing the freshly made chapatis onto a plate. She wiped her hands on her sari and moved closer to Arun, her voice lowering to a whisper. "You know your father," she said, her voice hushed. "His silence can be more telling than any words."

Arun looked away, feeling the familiar frustration rise within him. Silence. Always silent. Why couldn't Appa say what he thought and express how he felt? Arun would have preferred an argument, a confrontation, anything but this suffocating quiet that left him guessing.

"Aai," Arun said, his voice strained, "I don't understand him. He cherishes our traditions and everything he's taught me, but rejects anything new I try." I've tried to honor the past, but he makes it feel like I'm betraying him."

With a heavy heart from all the years, Vatsala sighed. "Your father wasn't always this way," she said softly, her eyes distant as if lost in a memory she hadn't revisited in years. "In his youth, he resembled you, brimming with ideas and dreams. But he also encountered resistance from his father. He tried to introduce something new, but he was met with harsh criticism. It's why he's so afraid now—to him, change is a risk he's not willing to take again."

Arun's expression softened slightly as the memory surfaced. He could still see himself as a small boy, watching in awe as his father carved delicate patterns into the wood, his hands steady and sure. Arun had idolized him back then, viewing him as a master of his craft—a man capable of transforming raw materials into beauty.

But those days felt distant now, almost like they belonged to someone else's life. The pride Ravji had once shown had faded, replaced by a wall of expectations Arun could no longer meet.

Vatsala placed a hand on his shoulder, her touch gentle but firm. "Your father loves you, Arun. He always has. But he's stubborn. He sees the world in a certain way, and change frightens him. It's not that he doesn't believe in you—he's afraid of what your work means for everything he's built."

Arun's frustration simmered beneath the surface, but Vatsala's words brought a measure of understanding he hadn't considered before. He could almost see it. Ravji's dreams were buried under the weight of tradition, the same weight he was now trying to place on Arun. Ravji wasn't just rejecting Arun's designs; he was clinging to the only way of life he knew, fearing that any deviation might threaten the legacy he had worked so hard to preserve.

Vatsala stepped back, glancing toward the door where Ravji had disappeared earlier. "Give him time, Arun. He needs to see that you're not trying to replace him. You're carrying forward his teachings in a way that speaks to the world today."

Arun nodded, though doubt still lingered in his mind. That was what everyone kept telling him. But how much time did it take for someone to heal old wounds? How long before Ravji saw that Arun's path wasn't a betrayal but a continuation of the dreams he once had himself?

As the night deepened, Ravji finally emerged from his room. His face remained as stern as ever, and his silence felt even more pronounced in the dim glow of the lamps. He sat at the table without a word, waiting for Vatsala to serve dinner. Arun watched him intently, searching for any clue, but Ravji remained impassive, his gaze fixed on his plate.

Vatsala glanced between the two men, her heart heavy with their unspoken conflict. She knew that tonight would not be the night for resolution, but she hoped, at least, to keep the peace. Quietly, she placed the food on the table, the warmth of the chapatis and dal filling the air.

For a few moments, there was nothing but the sound of utensils scraping against plates, the silence thick with unspoken words. Arun ached to break the oppressive silence, but his father's presence pressed down on him, stifling any attempt to speak.

It wasn't until Vatsala spoke again that the stillness was broken. "Ravji," she said softly, her voice measured, "did you see Arun's work at the fair today?"

Ravji looked up, his expression unreadable. For a long moment, he said nothing, and then finally, in a voice barely above a whisper, he muttered, "I saw it."

Vatsala waited, hoping for more, but Ravji offered no further words. The silence stretched once again, leaving Arun feeling more lost than ever. The confrontation he had feared hadn't come—but neither had the reconciliation he had hoped for.

So the rift between father and son remained, unresolved but ever-present, a silent force that threatened to tear their world apart.

The evening had passed in strained silence, with Vatsala quietly clearing away the dinner plates while Ravji and Arun avoided each other's eyes. The atmosphere in the small home was suffocating, thick with unspoken words. Arun could feel the weight of his father's disappointment pressing down on him, but he was too weary from the day's events to address it. Instead, he retreated to his small corner of the house, hoping that sleep would offer some reprieve.

But Ravji's thoughts churned like a storm inside him. He spent the evening mulling over the image of Arun's booth at the fair, where the modern designs attracted attention but clashed with the surrounding traditional pieces. Each intricate carving reminded him of the years he had dedicated to perfecting his craft, adhering strictly to the teachings passed down from his forefathers. The admiration Arun's work received was like a slap in the face, a reminder that the world was moving on, perhaps leaving him behind. As he watched his son's retreating figure, something inside Ravji snapped.

"Arun!" Ravji's voice cut through the stillness like a blade, sharp and unexpected.

Arun turned, surprised by the sudden outburst. He saw his father standing rigid, his face a mask of barely contained anger. The confrontation he had been dreading all day was finally here.

"What were you thinking?" Ravji demanded, his voice trembling with a mixture of fury and disbelief. His hands, usually so steady, clenched into fists at his sides. The sight of his son's work, so different from his own, had ignited a fear he struggled to contain—the fear that everything he had built was being cast aside. "How could you present those... those things and call them art? Have you forgotten everything I've taught you?"

A sweat line ran behind Arun's ears, and they burnt with anxiety as he faced his father. The accusations stung, but beneath the anger, he could sense Ravji's deeper fear—the gnawing dread of losing everything he had spent a lifetime building.

"They're not just things, Appa," Arun replied, trying to keep his voice steady. "They're my creations, a blend of what you taught me and what I see today. I'm not rejecting our heritage but trying to take it forward."

"Take it forward?" Ravji scoffed, his voice rising with each word. "By abandoning everything that makes our craft what it is? By turning your back on tradition? You're betraying our heritage, Arun! You're spitting on the legacy of our ancestors!"

The words landed like a punch to the gut, yet Arun refused to yield outwardly, even as his newfound confidence faltered under his father's anger.

"Appa, traditions aren't meant to stay frozen in time," Arun argued, his voice growing more impassioned. "They have to evolve, or they become irrelevant. I'm not rejecting what you've taught me—I'm building on it, making it something that speaks to people today. Isn't that what art is supposed to do? Speak to people?"

Ravji shook his head, the disbelief evident in his eyes. A memory surfaced—his youth when he had once dared to suggest a change to his father's method. He felt again the sting of the rebuke, the crushing humiliation of having his ideas dismissed, and the vow he made in the depths of his disappointment to never stray from tradition. But now, seeing Arun take the risks he had once feared, that old pain resurfaced, mixed with a desperate need to protect the legacy he had worked so hard to uphold.

"Art? You think what you're doing is art?" Ravji's voice was low, dangerous. "Art is what I've taught you—the intricate carvings, the careful attention to detail, and the respect for the wood and its natural form. What you're doing... it's a mockery!"

Arun sensed a surge of anger rise within him. He had poured his heart into creating a work that honored his heritage and dreams, yet his father dismissed it as a mockery. "It's not a mockery, Appa. It's a different direction, a way to keep our craft alive in a changing world. I'm trying to build on what you've given me, not tear it down."

But Ravji couldn't see it. All he could see was the fear growing inside him since Arun had started experimenting with new designs. Fear that everything he had worked for—everything his ancestors had worked for—was slipping away, lost to the whims of a younger generation that didn't understand the value of tradition.

"You think you know better than me?" Ravji's voice was tight, his hands gripping the table. "You think you can simply throw away everything I've taught you, everything our family stands for, and replace it with this?"

Arun's frustration boiled over. He had always tried to balance respect for his father's teachings with his need for expression, but this confrontation pushed him to the edge. "I'm not discarding anything! I'm trying to adapt to make something that will last beyond the walls of this town. Why can't you see that? Why can't you trust me?"

"Trust you?" Ravji's eyes flashed with anger. "How can I trust you when you're turning your back on everything I've tried to teach you? While you're dishonoring the traditions we've cherished for so long."

Arun's voice trembled with emotion as he shot back, "I'm not disrespecting it, Appa! I'm trying to make it relevant! What's the point of preserving something if no one cares about it anymore? We must adapt, or we risk becoming obsolete!"

The argument exploded, the two men facing each other, separated by only a few feet, yet a gulf of emotion separated their hearts. Arun's heart ached at the hurt and betrayal in his father's eyes. But he stood his ground; he couldn't back down with so much at stake.

Vatsala could no longer stay silent. She stepped forward, her voice gentle but firm as she tried to mediate the two men she loved most. "Listen to me," she began, her voice trembling slightly as she sought the right words, "please, both of you, stop this. Can't you see you're hurting each other? "Ravji, I understand how much our traditions mean to you—they mean everything to me too. Arun isn't rejecting our heritage; he's building upon it, ensuring its survival." But Arun is not trying to reject our heritage—he's trying to build on it, to make it something that will last."

Ravji's eyes flickered with doubt as he looked at Vatsala. She had always been the one to soothe his fears and truly understood the weight of their family's legacy. Her calm presence had always been his anchor, and now, as she spoke, he felt the storm inside him begin to subside, just a little.

"Isn't that what you've always wanted?" Vatsala continued, her gaze shifting to Arun. "For our family's legacy to live on? Arun's work… It's different, yes, but it's also beautiful. It carries the essence of what you've taught him, Ravji, but it also carries a piece of him—a piece of our future." She placed a hand on Ravji's arm, her touch calming. "Change is not always bad. Remember how different the world was when we were young? We can't hold on to the past forever. Arun is striving to take your teaching and adapt it for the future. Can't you see that? Can't you see that he's not trying to diminish our legacy but to add to it in his way?"

Vatsala's voice softened, her gaze holding both her husband and son. "Ravji, I've watched Arun grapple with this. He's not turning his back on you or our traditions; he's searching for a way to carry them forward into a new era. We know change is inevitable. But what you've instilled in him, Ravji will endure—if we allow it to evolve.

Ravji's shoulders drooped, the fire in his eyes fading slightly as Vatsala's words took hold. He looked at his son, really looked at him, and for the first time saw not just the defiance and frustration, but the passion and dedication that had driven Arun to create something new. In that moment, he saw a younger version of himself in Arun—the version that had once dared to dream beyond the boundaries his father had set. But the fear was still there, gnawing at him, whispering that if he let go, if he accepted this new direction, everything he had worked for would be lost.

Arun, seeing his father's hesitation, took a step forward. "Appa, I'm not asking you to give up everything you believe in. I'm asking you to let me find my way, to trust that what I'm doing is not a rejection of our past but a continuation of it. I want to make you proud, but I must stay true to myself. Can't we find a way to do both?"

Silence descended as Ravji considered his son's words. He looked down, then met Arun's gaze, finally seeing the depth of his conviction. The air crackled with anticipation, the silence thick enough to cut with a knife, as if the walls held their breath, awaiting his reply.

A heavy silence filled the room as Ravji weighed his son's words. His gaze shifted from the floor to Arun, and in that moment, he saw the unwavering conviction in his son's eyes. The tension in the room was palpable, as if the air held its breath, waiting for his decision.

Finally, Ravji spoke, his voice quiet and strained. "I don't know, Arun. I don't know if I can accept this... this change. I can see that you believe in it. And maybe... maybe that's enough, for now."

Vatsala felt a tear slip down her cheek—a tear of relief and gratitude. Though not a full reconciliation, this small, tentative step was a move toward understanding. She reached for Ravji's hand, squeezing it gently as she smiled at Arun, her eyes filled with mother's pride. Arun Nodding slowly, Arun's chest tightened with relief and unease, knowing the path to truly mending their bond was beginning. Yet, with his mother's support and the flicker of acceptance in his father's eyes, he felt a glimmer of hope—a hope that, in time, they could find a way to merge their worlds. For tonight, at least, the storm had passed, leaving behind the hope that, in time, they might find common ground.

As the tension in the room began to ease, Ravji's thoughts drifted back to a time when he had faced a similar crossroads. He remembered standing before his father, nervously presenting a new design he had spent weeks working on, hoping to modernize the traditional patterns passed down for generations. The rejection was swift and absolute, leaving him utterly crushed and convinced that tradition was untouchable. But now, as he looked at Arun, Ravji saw the same passion in his son's eyes that he had once felt—the same desire to innovate while still in the past, a desire he had buried deep within himself but one that he couldn't deny had once driven him.

The realization struck Ravji deeply: his fear wasn't just about losing tradition but Arun succeeding where he had failed. An inner conflict stirred within him, pitting his devotion to tradition against a grudging admiration for his son's courage. He wasn't ready to concede fully, but for the first time, he acknowledged that Arun's path wasn't necessarily wrong—just different.

Arun's heart swelled with emotions—relief, hope, and a lingering sadness for the struggle ahead. But his father's words, though tentative, were a breakthrough he hadn't expected. They were like a peace offering, a sign that the gap between them could be bridged with time and understanding.

Vatsala's smile widened as she saw the softening in Ravji's eyes, the first steps toward healing the rift that had threatened to tear their family apart. She understood the journey ahead would be arduous, filled with more conflict and pain, but a spark of hope ignited within her. That spark gave her the unwavering belief that they could find a path forward together.

The silence that followed wasn't heavy with tension anymore but with the quiet contemplation of what had been said and what had yet to be resolved. They still had a long journey ahead, but they had at least begun to find common ground, a language that embraced tradition and the inevitability of change.

That night, as Arun lay in bed, he thought about the conversation with his father. The confrontation had been painful, but it had also opened a door—a door to understanding and compromise. He still had much to prove, but the flicker of hope in Ravji's eyes gave him the strength to continue, knowing he wasn't alone in his journey.

In the stillness of their home, Ravji reflected. He wasn't ready to relinquish his fears entirely, but the seed of doubt had taken root, prompting him to question his rigid boundaries. Perhaps there was more than one path to preserving a legacy.

And so, as the night deepened and the household settled into a tentative peace, both father and son were left to ponder their next steps. The conflict was far from resolved, but the first steps had been taken. They both knew that tradition and innovation didn't have to be enemies—that, together, they might find a way to honor the past while embracing the future.

The next morning, the atmosphere in the workshop was silent, heavy with unspoken words. Even with Vatsala's attempt at mediation, the tension remained fragile, as if the slightest disturbance could break it apart. The once warm and familiar space, filled with the comforting scent of wood shavings and varnish, now felt stifling. The tools, once symbols of shared passion, now stood as silent, cold barriers between father and son.

Ravji stood at the workshop entrance, his fists clenched and his heart a tumultuous mix of anger and fear. Arun remained by the workbench, the familiar comfort of the space now tainted by the tension that hung heavy in the air. The soft glow of the evening lamps did little to ease the darkness that had settled between them.

Ravji's mind churned and caught between his love for Arun and the gnawing fear that all he and his ancestors had built was crumbling. The thought of Arun's modern designs, so different from the traditional ones that had been his life's work, gnawed at him like a persistent ache and wound that refused to heal. The silence between them grew heavier until Ravji couldn't bear it any longer.

"If you continue down this path, Arun," Ravji said in a low but firm voice, "you are no longer welcome in this workshop."

The words hung in the air, cold and final. Arun stared at his father, disbelief flashing across his face before it gave way to hurt. The workshop, which had always been a place of refuge and creation, now felt like a prison, with the walls closing in on him. He had expected resistance, even anger, but to be cast out of the place that had been his second home was a blow he hadn't anticipated.

"Appa, you don't mean that," Arun replied, his voice trembling with the weight of the situation. "This workshop... it's as much a part of me as it is of you. You taught me everything I know here."

Ravji's eyes softened, and then just as quickly, his grip tightened on the doorframe, regret chased away by a return to his hardened expression. In that fleeting moment, a memory surfaced—Ravji as a young man, standing before his father, nervously presenting a new design he had worked tirelessly on. The rejection had been swift, the words harsh, and the pain of that moment had never truly left him. Now, he was faced with his son, daring to tread the path he had once feared.

"I taught you the value of tradition and the importance of respecting the craft passed down through generations. If you can't appreciate the importance of our heritage, you're no longer welcome here."

Arun's heart ached at his father's words. The tools—the knives, saws, gauges, each carefully arranged—now mocked him, relics of a past he was accused of betraying. The workshop, once a sanctuary where he'd discovered his passion and learned under Ravji's watchful eye, now felt like a part of himself being torn away.

But Arun couldn't deny the pull of his vision, his desire to create something new and meaningful. The praise he had received at the art fair reverberated in his mind, a constant reminder of the world beyond the workshop walls—a world starting to acknowledge his talent.

"If that is how you feel, then there is nothing I can do, Appa," Arun uttered, feeling intense emotion in his throat. His voice was steady, but his heart felt heavy as he made the painful decision. "I'll leave."

Ravji didn't respond immediately. His face was a mask of stoic resolve, but inside, his heart twisted with the knowledge of what his words had done. The tools that had once represented their shared heritage now felt like a burden, tethering him to a fading past that he feared Arun might abandon. He watched as Arun turned to gather his tools, the familiar clatter of metal against wood ironically out of place in the tense atmosphere.

Vatsala stood at the doorway, her hands clasped tightly together, her eyes wide with concern. "Her worst fear had come true, and it hurt more than she could have imagined." She wanted to intervene, to say something that would mend the rift between her husband and son, but the words failed her. The tools and materials that had once filled the room with the promise of creation now felt like instruments of destruction, tearing the family apart. Torn between her husband and son's conflicting emotions, she felt a deep connection to them both.

Arun methodically packed his tools. Each one evoked memories of learning at his father's side: the first touch of a chisel, Ravji's patient guidance, and the late nights spent crafting pieces meant to carry their legacy forward. Those memories now felt distant, eclipsed by the harsh present.

There was a moment of hesitation as Arun picked up the last tool—a small carving knife that Ravji had given him when he was just a boy. He held it, its weight familiar, recalling his father's pride when he first learned to use it. The knife, a symbol of their bond, now felt heavy with the burden of unspoken words and unresolved conflict. Arun's grip tightened around the handle, and for a brief moment, he considered staying or trying one last time to reach an understanding.

But the memory of Ravji's words—"You are no longer welcome"—was a fresh wound. Arun took a deep breath, carefully placed the knife in his bag, and closed it.

Ravji watched every movement, his heart heavy with the weight of unspoken words, torn between his pride and the deep love he felt for his son. Every part of him wanted to apologize, but his pride held him back. He had drawn the line, and stepping back now would feel like a betrayal of everything he believed in. As he watched Arun leave, a small part of him longed to reach out, to say something that would bridge the growing divide, but the words remained trapped in his throat.

With the weight of his decision pressing down on him, Arun slung his bag over his shoulder and turned to face his father one last time. He searched Ravji's face for any sign of softening, any indication that there was still hope for reconciliation.

But Ravji's expression remained unreadable, a mask of hardened resolve that barely concealed the turmoil beneath. Arun's heart sank as he realized words wouldn't change his father's mind.

"Goodbye, Appa," Arun said quietly, his voice laced with sorrow and determination.

Ravji didn't respond; his silence was more painful than any words could have been. As Arun turned to leave, Ravji noticed the carving knife his son had left behind—the same one he had given him as a boy. The sight of it stirred something within him—a flicker of doubt that perhaps he had been too hasty, too harsh. Arun turned and walked out of the workshop, his footsteps echoing in the stillness. With each step, he felt himself drifting further away from his familiar life, heading into an uncertain future.

Vatsala watched Arun leave, her heart shattering with the certainty that the divide between him and his father had grown even deeper. She wanted to comfort Arun but knew he needed to face this alone. Instead, she turned to Ravji, her eyes pleading for him to intervene, to mend the rift between them.

Ravji remained silent, his eyes fixed on the empty doorway where Arun had just disappeared. His heart ached with the knowledge of what he had lost, but his pride kept him rooted to the spot, unable to reach out. Yet as he stood there, the weight of the chisel in his hand flickered within him—hope that perhaps, one day, there might still be a way to mend what had been broken.

As Arun left the workshop, the familiar town seemed distant and hazy. The weight of his decision—a mix of freedom and regret—pressed down on him. He had defended his vision but lost his mentor, guide, and father.

But even as he walked away, the memory of Ravji's gaze lingering on the carving knife stayed with him—a small, almost imperceptible gesture that hinted at something deeper—a possibility that their bond, though strained, was not entirely severed.

Determined to prove himself, Arun walked on, the rift weighing heavily on his heart. But with each step, he knew there was no turning back. This was his path now, and he would have to walk it alone. Yet, deep within, he held onto a fragile hope. One day, their paths might converge again—not in opposition but in harmony, blending tradition and innovation into something greater than either could achieve alone.

CHAPTER FOUR

A New Beginning

The scent of fresh wood and the promise of endless possibilities filled Arun's new workshop, a modest space with bare, unpolished walls. But the echoes in that space spoke not only of potential but also of the uncertainties ahead. The soft light filtering through the small windows cast a serene, almost sacred glow—a stark counterpoint to the turmoil churning within Arun: fear, hope, and a lingering sense of loss. Here, stepping out from his father's shadow, he would define his future.

Bharat had been instrumental in making this new beginning a reality. After the explosive argument and Arun's subsequent exit from the family workshop, Bharat had been unwavering in his support. "You can't stay adrift," Bharat had declared. "I'll help you find a new beginning."

It had taken days of searching, but Bharat had finally found this old, unused storeroom at the edge of the town. It was tucked away behind a small shop, its door barely visible through the overgrown weeds. The space was far from perfect, but it had potential. Bharat had convinced the shop owner to lease it to Arun, negotiating terms that were generous considering the condition of the place.

The day they moved in, Bharat arrived early with a heavy toolbox. "This place has charm, Arun. A bit rough around the edges, but just like you—full of promise," he said, placing the toolbox on the floor with a thud.

Arun offered a faint smile, a thin veil over the deep ache in his heart from the past few days. The weight of his father's rejection pressed on him like a hammer, but he forced himself to see the potential in this new space. "It's not much, but it's a start," he replied, running his fingers over a piece of raw wood. "I can finally create without looking over my shoulder."

Bharat nodded, understanding the weight of those words. "You've always been meant for this. Now, you can do it on your terms."

As they unpacked, Bharat's voice drifted into a nostalgic recollection. "Remember when we were kids and you'd draw designs in your notebooks?" Ravji-uncle would catch you and scold you for wasting time, but then you'd sneak off to the workshop and try to bring those sketches to a craft."

Arun chuckled; the memory brought a smile to his face. "I remember. I'd stay up late, hoping to impress him, hoping he'd see that I could do more than follow his methods." The memory, however, quickly turned bittersweet, a reminder of the unspoken expectations that had always hung between them.

"But he did see it, Arun. In his way," Bharat replied, placing a reassuring hand on Arun's shoulder. "He was too proud to admit that his son might outshine him."

Arun sighed, the memories bittersweet. "Maybe. But was it pride or fear that held him back? Did he see me as a continuation of his legacy or a threat?" He shook his head, dispelling the thought. "Now, I have to prove to myself that I can do this—without his approval and guidance."

Their conversation was interrupted by the creaking sound of the door. Saavitri, Damodar's wife, entered with a basket of food and supplies. Her presence was quiet yet comforting—a silent acknowledgement of support.

"Arun," she greeted with a warm smile, handing him the basket. "You'll need your strength if you build something different here."

"Thank you, Kaki," Arun replied, surprised but grateful. This small gesture reminded him that he was not as alone as he felt, even though he had expected to face this journey alone. "It means a lot that you'd do this."

She looked around the workshop, her eyes lingering on the half-finished scattered pieces. "Damodar doesn't know I'm here," she said softly, a hint of mischief in her tone. "But he respects you, even if he won't say it. Keep working, Arun. This is your calling." Arun's heart swelled with gratitude and determination, her words reigniting the spark of resolve he had felt slipping away.

As Savitri left, the room filled with quiet determination. Arun felt a flicker of hope—small, but enough to keep him moving forward. He wasn't alone in this journey, even if the path was uncertain and strewn with doubts.

Later that evening, Arun sat alone, reflecting on the day after Bharat and Savitri Kaki had left and the workshop fell silent. His thoughts drifted back to when he and his father worked side by side, the memory vivid as if it had happened just yesterday.

The rhythmic sound of chisels on wood filled the air as Arun, a young apprentice then, worked diligently beside Ravji. His father, with the precision of a master, guided his hands, teaching him the intricate details of traditional carving. The boy's eyes sparkled with admiration as he mimicked each stroke, eager to please his father.

"That's it, Arun," Ravji's gruff voice filled with pride. "You've got the skill, but you need the patience. A true craftsman knows that perfection can't be rushed."

Rare praise from his father filled Arun with joy, forging a deep connection between them. In those moments, the workshop became a sacred space where their shared love for the craft bound them together, transcending time. He longed to recreate this bond, even as he forged his path.

Now, sitting in his workshop, the memory was a bittersweet reminder of their once-strong bond. Tension and conflict had replaced their shared connection, yet a part of Arun still craved the approval that had been so elusive.

But as Arun looked around his new space, he realised that this was his chance to honour his father's teachings in a way that was true to himself.

He picked up a gouge, its curved blade catching the light as he cradled the wood block in his other hand. The familiar weight of the tool grounded him, connecting him to his craft and heritage. "This is my beginning," he whispered to the empty room, the words both a declaration and a plea. "I will create something worthy of our name.

As the night deepened, carving filled the workshop, blending old techniques with new ideas, echoing the promise of reconciliation—someday.

Arun sat in his workshop late into the evening, the soft glow of the oil lamp casting long shadows on the walls. The space was almost too quiet, leaving him alone with his thoughts. He reached for one of his father's old carvings, a small but intricate piece that had always stood on the highest shelf in the family workshop. The craftsmanship was flawless; every line and curve was a testament to Ravji's skill and dedication. As Arun turned the piece over in his hands, he felt a familiar mixture of awe and trepidation.

"How will Appa react to my new work?" Arun pondered, his chest constricting from the burden of expectation. Though he was terrified of disappointing his father, he was also clinging to the hope that his inventions would win Ravji's acceptance. But was that hope realistic? Would his father see his new direction as a betrayal of the craft he had so carefully preserved, or could he understand that Arun's path was not about abandoning tradition but carrying it forward in a new light?

Questions hammered at Arun as he set the carving back on the shelf, a deep sigh escaping his lips. He felt the fragility of his bond with his father; it threatened to shatter under any pressure. The stakes were high; he couldn't risk alienating Ravji. Yet, despite the fear, Arun knew he couldn't turn back. This was his journey, and he had to walk it—even if it meant alone.

The next evening, the quiet of Arun's workshop was broken by the arrival of a man in a tailored suit and polished shoes. The contrast between the visitor's sharp attire and the humble surroundings struck Arun as almost surreal. Arun, so engrossed in shaping the piece of wood, didn't notice him at first. The visitor cleared his throat, a sound that seemed almost too refined for the rustic workshop.

Arun looked up, his eyes widening in surprise at the sight of the man standing before him. The visitor radiated an aura of confidence and significance, yet his gaze held a warmth that made Arun feel at ease.

"Good evening, Arun," the man began, extending his hand with a smile. "Prashant Chavan. I had the pleasure of seeing your work at the art fair."

Arun's eyes widened in surprise, a rush of shock and happiness coursing through him. He quickly cleaned his hands with his apron before handshake. "Mr. Chavan?" he stammered, his voice betraying his excitement. "I... I can't believe you're here—in my workshop! It's an honour, sir.

Prashant's eyes roamed the workshop, taking in the scattered tools, the half-finished pieces, and the scent. of fresh wood. "I was quite impressed by the fusion of traditional techniques with modern design in your work," he said, his tone both appreciative and businesslike. "It's rare to see such a seamless blend of the old and the new."

Arun's heart raced, a mixture of excitement and trepidation. "Thank you, sir. That means a lot," he said, though his mind was already racing ahead to the implications of this encounter.

Prashant smiled, a mix of warmth and keen interest. "I'm here with a proposal, Arun. I'd like you to work on a project for me that embodies the blend of tradition and innovation that I saw in your work at the fair."

The opportunity was extraordinary—a chance to gain recognition and secure his career. But it also meant embracing a path that had already caused tension with his father. Ravji's disapproval loomed over him like a shadow, casting doubt on this promising moment. Arun's mind was filled with images of his father's stern face and the disappointment in his eyes whenever Arun strayed from the traditional methods.

Prashant continued, "This project will be high-profile. It's not just about craftsmanship but making a statement. And I believe you're the right person for this."

Arun envisioned a design that honoured traditional methods and boldly pushed their boundaries. The idea was exhilarating, yet the potential fallout with his father made the decision difficult. He could almost hear Ravji's voice, cautioning him against abandoning the old ways. The thought made his heart pound with anxiety.

Prashant noticed Arun's hesitation and took a step closer, his tone turning more personal. "This is a big decision, especially with your father's legacy. But this project—this could be your breakthrough. This is how you make your mark. It's an opportunity to show that tradition and innovation don't have to be at odds."

Arun met Prashant's gaze, the weight of the moment pressing down on him. His father's validation had always been a guiding force, and the thought of further straining their relationship was almost unbearable. But there was also a pull within him, a desire to prove his vision was valid.

I appreciate your confidence in me, Mr. Chavan," Arun stated, his voice steady, a flicker of doubt quickly masked by resolve. "This is a significant step, and I need to think about how I can approach it in a way that respects both the old and the new."

Prashant nodded with understanding. "Take the time you need. But know this: opportunities like this are rare." I'm confident you'll find a way to make this work, Arun. And when you do, it will be something extraordinary."

The weight of the decision settled on Arun's shoulders. The thrill of creation was intoxicating, yet the fear of alienating his father gnawed at him. Unconsciously, his grip tightened on the chisel, seeking solace in the familiar tool. He hesitated his thoughts, a whirlwind of conflicting emotions. "I'll give you my decision soon, Mr. Chavan," he finally said, his voice tinged with determination and doubt. "I want to make sure that whatever I create is something we can both be proud of."

Prashant smiled, clearly pleased with Arun's response. "I look forward to hearing from you. I'm sure you'll find the right balance, Arun. And when you do, it will be a piece that will resonate with many."

With a final handshake, Prashant left the workshop, leaving Arun to grapple with the weight of his decision. The future of his craft and his relationship with his father hung in the balance, but Arun knew one thing for certain—he was ready to take the next step, wherever it might lead.

The clinking of tea cups accompanied Arun's restless pacing. His hands clenched into fists as he moved back and forth, his eyes darting nervously around the room.

"You're thinking about the project, aren't you?" Bharat asked, pouring another cup of tea.

Arun nodded, his eyes fixed on some distant point. "I know, Bharat. It's a huge opportunity, but it comes at a cost. Taking it means distancing myself even further from Appa."

Bharat leaned forward, his expression earnest. Noticing Arun's nervous fingers, he said, "This is your chance to prove you can evolve our traditions while staying true to yourself."

Arun sighed, his conflict intense. His father's words echoed in his mind, warning against losing their heritage to the whims of modernity. But deep down, Arun knew that change was inevitable. "But what if this decision widens the gap between him and his father? What if he sees it as a betrayal?"

Bharat placed a reassuring hand on Arun's shoulder, his touch grounding. "Your father loves you, Arun. He may not understand your vision now, but he will come around. You have to trust in your journey. Remember, you're not rejecting tradition—you're building on it, taking it to new heights."

Arun didn't respond immediately, eyes lingering on the mallet on the table. He picked it up, feeling the familiar weight in his hand, and stared at it for a long moment, lost in thought. The silence between them was heavy, filled with the unspoken fears that neither wanted to voice. Arun tightened his grip on the mallet, a gesture that spoke volumes about the turmoil within him. "I hope you're right, Bharat," he finally whispered, though the doubt lingered in his voice.

Arun thought back to Saarika Desai's words at the art fair. Her praise had been a beacon of encouragement, confirming that he was on the right path. He recalled her smile and her enthusiasm as she spoke about his work.

At Arun's booth, Saarika's eyes shone with curiosity. "Your work," she observed, "is more than mere craftsmanship. It's a unique blend of tradition and innovation, a testament to a deep understanding of both. You're doing something extraordinary here."

Arun had felt a surge of hope at her words, a reassurance that his vision had value. But now that hope was tinged with doubt. He wondered if Saarika's words would still ring true if she knew the cost of pursuing that vision.

Arun gazed around his new workshop, a blank canvas awaiting his vision. The bare walls whispered of endless possibilities. This wasn't merely a project; it was an opportunity to define himself and to reconcile his artistic spirit with his filial duty. Accepting Prashant's offer meant embracing the unknown, but it also meant embracing his becoming.

Arun drew a deep breath, his resolve strengthening. "You're right, Bharat. This is the path I need to take. It's a risk with a chance to create something extraordinary by uniting tradition and innovation."

Bharat smiled, seeing the determination in his friend's eyes. "You're destined for greatness, Arun. I have faith in you."

Arun nodded, a newfound confidence washing over him. The project from Prashant Chavan was more than just a job—a challenge—an opportunity to bridge the gap between the old and the new and to prove that his vision wasn't just valid but essential.

But as Arun made his way to the town post office, where the public telephone stood, a final wave of doubt swept over him. He hesitated, his fingers hovering over the dial. What if this decision pushed his father away for good? What if, in choosing this path, he lost something even more valuable?

After battling fear and opportunity through a restless night, Arun found himself back at the post office the following morning. Arun gripped the phone tightly at the post office, his breath catching as he dialled Prashant's number. An eternity of rings ended when Prashant's warm, hopeful voice sparked a surge of determination within Arun.

"Mr. Chavan, this is Arun. I've made my decision," he began, his voice steady. "I'm accepting your project. Let's create something extraordinary together."

Prashant's laughter boomed through the phone. "I knew you wouldn't disappoint me, Arun. This is the right move. Get ready—this is going to be huge." The agreement with Prashant was poised to transform Arun's career: he would craft a distinctive series of sculptures, fusing modern design with traditional architectural elements. In exchange, Prashant would showcase Arun's work in Mumbai's top galleries and introduce him to influential collectors and investors. This pivotal moment marked a turning point, granting him access to a wider market while preserving his artistic integrity.

As Arun hung up the phone, he felt excitement and trepidation. He had taken the plunge, but the water was still deep and murky. The path ahead was uncertain, but it was his path. With Bharat's support and encouragement, Arun knew he was ready to walk it.

This moment marked a turning point in Arun's journey—a decisive commitment to his chosen path, despite the inherent risks. The project was not just a test of his craftsmanship but a challenge to his very identity, his connection to his father, and the legacy he sought to redefine. With that decision, Arun began a new chapter that would redefine the intersection of tradition and innovation.

A pleasant morning greeted Arun; a gentle breeze stirred the air, energising him as he stepped into his modest, new workshop. Unlike the shared space with his father, this workshop was his own—a sanctuary he had built to forge his path. Yet, even here, the echoes of unspoken words and unresolved tension followed him. The air was filled with the familiar scent of varnish and wood, but instead of being comforting, it held expectations he was still getting used to. Even in this new space, the silence between him and his father lingered, a heavy presence clinging to the walls.

Seeking refuge in the rhythmic sound of his chisel, Arun worked with a focus that became almost meditative. The steady tap-tap against the wood was a small escape, allowing him to drown out the doubts creeping into his mind. Sunlight filtered softly through the windows, casting a warm glow that momentarily brought life to the space. Yet, beneath this calm exterior, Arun's heart was restless, weighed down by the events of recent days. Though he was physically distant from his father, the weight of tradition and his father's presence seemed to linger, questioning his every step forward.

A soft knock at the door pulled Arun from his focused work. He wiped the beads of sweat from his brow and called, "Come in."

His mother entered, carrying a small, weathered wooden box. Though her presence was usually a comfort, an unexpected apprehension washed over Arun. She moved silently to the bench, her sari barely brushing the floor. Arun's heart gave a jolt—a flood of surprise and curiosity.

"Aai," he greeted her with a gentle voice and teary eyes. "What brings you here?"

Aai smiled, her smile holding a thousand unspoken words. Her eyes, however, were tinged with something deeper—a mix of pride, sorrow, and implied understanding. She placed the box on the bench, her fingers lingering on the worn wood for a moment before she spoke. "I found these in the old storeroom," she said softly.

Arun's eyes widened as she opened the box, revealing a set of old tools—chisels, carving knives, and other implements, their handles smooth from years of use. He recognised them instantly; these were the tools Ravji had used in his youth before the weight of tradition settled on his shoulders. Aai nodded, a mixture of pride and sadness softening her gaze. "Yes. These tools were with him through it all, shaping his finest work. Simple tools, yet capable of enduring beauty."

She paused, her gaze softening as she looked around the workshop, taking in the familiar sights that had once been a part of her daily life. "You know, Arun," she began, her voice carrying a note of reminiscence, "when your father and I were first married, he was much like you—full of ideas, eager to bring something new to the craft. But he struggled too. He envisioned a fusion of knowledge and imagination—a new technique. But his father, a staunch traditionalist, resisted fiercely.

Ravji was torn, just like you are now. He wanted to honour his father, but he also felt a pull to innovate, to create something that was uniquely his."

Arun listened intently, his hands still resting on the tools, as his mother continued. "Ultimately, he opted to adhere to tradition, possibly driven by respect or fear. Yet, I believe he always carried a sense of what might have been if he had followed his path. "I see in you the same spark and determination Ravji had. But you have a chance to do what he couldn't—to respect our past and build something innovative."

A heavy silence fell, laden with unspoken emotions. In that moment, Arun felt the weight of generations—the unbroken lineage of tradition embodied by these tools. Aai's gaze met Arun's, and for a moment, they were just mother and son, connected by the love they both held for Ravji, despite the rift that had grown between them.

"Why are you giving these to me?" Arun asked, his voice barely above a whisper. The question carried more than just curiosity—it was laden with trepidation and self-doubt, as he questioned whether he was truly worthy of this legacy and could ever live up to it.

Aai hesitated, choosing her words carefully. "Your father... he never said it, but he was proud of you and your skills and dedication, Arun. He may not understand your path, but that doesn't mean he doesn't respect it. These tools—they're a part of him, a part of our family's legacy. They could be a part of your work too."

A lump rose in Arun's throat as he absorbed the weight of her words. A wave of emotions crashed over him—gratitude, relief, and a deep-seated fear that he might still disappoint the man whose approval he had always sought. With tearful eyes, tools and Aai looked blurred, and he nodded slowly.

"I am so grateful, Aai. This means more to me than you know.," his voice gruffed with emotion.

Aai placed a gentle hand on his shoulder, her touch warm and reassuring. "Beta, I've seen how hard you've worked and always believed in you," she said softly. "Prashant Chavan's name carries weight, but your talent is what truly shines. You deserve this."

Arun swallowed the lump in his throat, hesitating before continuing, "I'm working on a project for Prashant. " It's for the cultural centre he's building, and this is my opportunity to demonstrate my abilities to the world."

Aai smiled, her eyes sparkling with pride. "You're making us all proud. Your father will also acknowledge it, eventually."

Her words, a quiet balm to his anxiety, lingered in the air as Arun realised this wasn't just about the project. It was about believing in himself, with his family standing by his side.

Vatsala smiled again, a hint of sadness in her eyes. She reached out to touch his cheek. "Just remember, Arun, tradition isn't about doing things the way they've always been done. It's about knowing where you come from, even as you forge your path."

With that, Vatsala reached into the folds of her sari and pulled out a small, neatly wrapped parcel. "I made your favourite—Puran Poli," she said softly, placing the warm package on the bench beside the tools. The rich, familiar aroma of the sweet dish filled the room, stirring memories of simpler times when the family would sit together and share meals, laughter, and stories. Arun's eyes welled up, overwhelmed by her kindness.

"Aai," he began, his voice breaking, "you didn't have to..."

"I wanted to," Vatsala said gently, her voice trembling slightly. "I know how much you've been burdened, and I wanted to reassure you: I'm here for you, always."

Arun's gaze shifted from the Puran Poli to his mother, his heart overflowing at this simple, profound gesture of love. "Thank you, Aai," he whispered, his voice thick with emotion. "Your support means everything to me, Aai."

With that, she turned and moved lightly toward the door. Before stepping out, she paused and looked back at him. "Your father... he's stubborn, but he loves you. Give him time." Her words hung in the air, offering comfort and a reminder of the unresolved tension between father and son.

After the door closed behind her, Arun stood staring at the tools. The place, once vibrant with shared work, now felt suspended between past and future, heavy with unspoken decisions. But as he held the chisel, the room seemed to lighten, the act of creation breathing life back into the strained silence.

The chisel in his hand was more than just a tool—a bridge between the legacy he was born into and the path he was carving for himself. He returned to his workbench, the chisel in hand, and began to carve.

His hands moved with a new awareness guided not by his skill but by the memories of his father's teachings. But this time, his movements were slower, more deliberate. He wasn't just working with wood; he was working with memories, with the legacy his father had passed down to him. With each stroke, Arun felt both the weight of his father's expectations and the freedom to forge his path. The tools, once symbols of rigid tradition, now bridge the divide between the old and the new. It seemed like the tools themselves were guiding him, reminding him of the lessons he had learnt from his father. The strokes became smoother and more confident as the design began to shape—a fusion of old and new, tradition and innovation. The piece that emerged was unlike anything Arun had created. before, yet it felt right as if it was exactly what he was meant to make. At that moment, Arun realised that he wasn't just creating a new piece; he was crafting a new beginning that could hold the possibility of reconciliation.

Arun's shoulders straightened, a determined glint in his eyes. He experienced a sense of purpose settled deep within him. Reconciliation remained uncertain but no longer impossible. With each stroke, he carved not just a new design but a new beginning—one that held the promise of healing for himself and his family.

Arun straightened his shoulders, a glint of determination in his eyes. A sense of purpose, not merely hope, surged through him for the first time in weeks. Reconciliation was still a distant prospect, but it no longer felt beyond reach. With each stroke, he carved more than just a design; he carved a new beginning—a chance for healing for himself and his family.

CHAPTER FIVE

A Bridge Between Eras

The days blurred together in the workshop. Arun worked tirelessly, pouring all his energy into Prashant's project. The pressure was immense. This wasn't just another job; it was a chance to prove himself, to show his father and the world what he was truly capable of.

As he carved, a memory surfaced—the time his experiment had failed. The disappointment in his father's eyes, the silent judgment, still stung. Now, the same fear gnawed at him. What if he failed again?

The next morning, Arun visited the town elder, Ganpat, whose wisdom had guided generations of craftsmen. Arun approached the elder's home with anticipation and trepidation, carrying the sketches that had consumed his thoughts. The elder, a man of few words but deep insight, welcomed him into the cool shade of his veranda. Laying out his plans, Arun hesitated, feeling the weight of his questions. 'What do you think, Kaka?' he asked, hoping for reassurance.

Ganpat studied the sketches in silence, his seasoned fingers tracing the lines as if sensing the essence of the designs. After a long pause, Ganpat nodded slowly. "This path demands courage, Arun," he said, "and your courage will be your greatest strength." Ganpat's gaze held Arun's. "Our craft is a matter not only of skill but of spirit. Honor that, and your work will speak for itself.' The elder's words echoed in Arun's mind long after he left, offering comfort yet deepening the gravity of his task.

As Arun walked back to his workshop with a sense of accomplishment, whispers followed him as he navigated through the bustling stalls. 'He's adding modern touches to our traditions,' a townfolk muttered, a note of disapproval in his voice. 'He'll ruin everything,' another agreed, shaking his head. Arun felt the sting of their words, the doubt creeping back into his thoughts. But then, as he passed a group of younger townfolk, he caught snippets of a different conversation. 'Maybe it's time for something new,' one murmured, her voice tinged with curiosity and hope. 'I've seen his work before—it's beautiful and respectful,' another added, eyes shining with admiration. The community's mixed reactions—skepticism and support—strengthened Arun's resolve and deepened his understanding of the delicate balance he had to maintain.

The workshop was in disarray. Scraps of wood, discarded sketches, and unused tools littered the floor, marking Arun's restless attempts to capture a design that felt just out of reach. He often worked late into the night, his mind a tumultuous mix of determination and doubt. But as the wooden block slipped through the benchhook, Arun paused. Was this project truly about innovation, or was he trying to prove something to his father and the town? The doubt gnawed at him—was he creating from his heart or from a need to be seen and validated? The lamp's light shone on his messy workspace and the deep lines on his forehead—showing how hard he'd been working. Short bursts of good ideas gave him quick moments of success, but then waves of doubt came and made him question everything he did.

Arun experimented with a new technique, hoping to merge the clean lines of modern design with the intricate patterns of traditional carving. But as the carving knife met the wood, it splintered under the pressure, shattering the delicate balance he sought to maintain. He cursed softly, frustration bubbling as he wiped the sweat from his brow.

In the afternoon, the workshop door creaked open as Arun stood over a particularly uncooperative piece of wood, his hands hurting from the effort. He looked up to see Fakira, the retired carpenter and his mentor from his apprenticeship days, standing in the doorway. Fakira's weathered face broke into a gentle smile as he entered, his presence bringing calm to the chaotic workshop.

"Arun," Fakira greeted, his voice warm and steady. "You're working yourself too hard, my boy."

Before Arun could answer, Meera stepped up behind Fakira. The town potter and a dear friend, Meera, carried herself with quiet strength. Her vibrant sari splashed color against her clay-stained hands. Her pottery feels connected directly to the earth, infused with her spirit.

"Look at you, Arun," Meera said, her eyes twinkling with concern and amusement. "You're drowning in sawdust and sketches. When was the last time you took a break?"

Arun sighed, wiping the sweat from his brow. "I don't have a choice, Meera. This project... it's everything."

Fakira nodded, his eyes scanning the workshop. "This is good," he said, picking up one of the sketches. "But it feels... affected. Like you're trying too much to impress someone."

As Fakira's eyes moved from sketch to sketch, Arun felt rapid heartbeats. He could see the skepticism in his mentor's gaze. Was he pushing too far? The fear that he might lose what made the craft special gnawed at him—was this innovation or just a dangerous gamble?

Arun winced at the truth in Fakira's words. "It's just... I need this to be perfect. I need to prove that I can do this—that I can blend the old with the new without losing what makes our craft special."

"Perfection is a dangerous trap, Arun," Meera said, stepping closer. "Art isn't about perfection; it's about expression. You've always been at your best when you let your heart guide your hands. Why are you trying so hard to fit into someone else's idea of what your work should be?"

Fakira chuckled softly, his eyes twinkling with wisdom. "Perfection is a myth, Arun. What you need to focus on is honesty. Be true to your vision, but don't forget where you come from.

Tradition isn't just about the techniques. we use; it's about the stories we tell through our work. Your designs need to speak to both the past and the future."

Before Arun could respond, the workshop door opened again, revealing Kavya, a young apprentice from the town learning the craft under Arun's guidance. Her bright, eager eyes took in the scene, and she quickly set down a basket of fresh fruits she had brought.

"Arun Bhaiya," Kavya said, her voice tinged with concern, "you haven't eaten anything today. I thought you might need some energy."

Arun smiled gratefully at the young girl. Kavya's enthusiasm reminded him of himself at her age, when he would eagerly soak up every lesson his father had to offer. Her presence reminded him of his responsibility to his legacy and those who followed him.

"Thank you, Kavya," Arun said, taking a custard apple from the basket. "I've been so caught up in this project that I forgot to take care of myself."

Kavya's eyes flickered over the sketches spread across the table. "These designs... they're beautiful, Bhaiya. But they seem so different from what you usually do. Why are you changing your style?"

Arun paused, the custard apple halfway to his mouth. "Because I need to show that I can innovate, Kavya. But sometimes, I wonder if I'm losing myself."

Meera shared a knowing look with Fakira. "Arun," she said, "innovation isn't about discarding your roots. It's about growing from them, about carrying forward the heart of what you've learned. Remember that innovation without a soul is just a fleeting trend. Your work's soul is its enduring power."

Fakira placed a hand on Arun's shoulder, his grip firm and reassuring. "You won't lose the soul if you remember it's already a part of you. Your father's legacy lives on in your hands, guiding every stroke of the chisel.

As Arun carved, he could hear his father's voice in his mind, a constant reminder of the discipline and precision required. Every stroke carried the weight of Ravji's teachings, and as much as Arun wanted to innovate, he couldn't deny the comfort of following those familiar patterns. But was he honoring his father's legacy, or was he too afraid to break free?

This is your journey now, Arun. You have to find your way, just as Ravji did. It's not about choosing one or the other, but finding the balance between them."

Arun's gaze swept across the faces of those closest to him—Fakira, his wise mentor; Meera, his steadfast friend; and Kavya, his eager apprentice. Their belief in him helped him rediscover his original purpose. A clarity he hadn't felt in days washed over him.

"Thank you, all of you." His voice was filled with gratitude as he expressed his appreciation. "I needed to hear that more than I realized."

As the three of them left the workshop, Arun was energized with a renewed sense of purpose. He picked up the tools his mother had brought him—the ones that had once belonged to his father. Arun's hands moved almost unconsciously, following the patterns his father had taught him. But this time, he allowed his ideas to flow, blending the old with the new naturally, even inevitable. He could almost feel Ravji's presence, not as a shadow but as a guide, leading him toward a harmony he had long sought. The weight of the tools in his hands was comforting, a reminder of the skills and knowledge passed down through generations.

Later that evening, Vatsala quietly entered the workshop, the soft rustle of her sari the only sound. Lost in thought, Arun didn't notice her until the familiar scent of jasmine—a constant reminder of her presence—gently drew him back. "Arun," Vatsala's voice was soft yet carried a mother's deep concern. He looked up, surprised to see her so late.

"Aai," he said, his voice tinged with exhaustion. "What are you doing here? It's late; you should be resting."

Vatsala shook her head and gave him a small, tender smile. "I couldn't sleep, knowing you were here, pushing yourself hard." She brushed a lock of hair from his forehead, a silent reassurance passing between them. "You've always been like this, even as a child—so determined, so focused. But you carry too much weight on your shoulders, my son."

Arun's eyes softened, the tension in his brow easing slightly. "I just want to make something that would make you and Appa proud," he admitted, his voice betraying the vulnerability he rarely showed.

Vatsala's eyes filled with a deep, unspoken understanding. Vatsala understood his struggle—the desire to honour his father's legacy battling the fear of unmet expectations. She took his hand in hers, squeezing it gently. "Arun, we've always been proud of you. Not just for what you create, but for the man you've become. You are not alone in this. Your father's love, my love, it's all here with you, in every stroke you make."

His mother's words brought a long-awaited release, easing the deep-seated tension that had plagued him for days. He lowered his gaze, the depth of her words sinking in. "But what if I can't do it, Aai? What if I fail?"

Vatsala lifted his chin, meeting his gaze. "You won't fail, Arun. Not because of perfection, but because you're pouring your heart into this. We want you to follow your dreams, Arun. Be yourself."

Her touch on his shoulder brought a wave of calm, soothing the turmoil within. "Your father may not say it, but he's proud of you," she whispered, her voice filled with quiet conviction. "And so am I. Remember, son, the heart of the craft lies in the soul. Let that guide you." Arun looked into his mother's eyes. seeing the depth of her love and understanding, and felt a renewed sense of calm wash over him.

Before Arun could respond, Vatsala handed him a small, intricately carved box. "This was your grandfather's," she said softly, her voice filled with longing. "He passed it on to your father when he first embarked on his journey. I think it's time it became part of your journey." Arun felt the weight of the box in his hands, its smooth surface worn by time and history. As he opened the lid, revealing a set of finely crafted tools, he understood the significance of what his mother was passing on to him. More than just a box, it represented a connection to the past and a symbol of the legacy he was now a part of. This simple act anchored him to his past even as he shaped his future.

With his mother's words and the legacy of his ancestors in his heart, Arun sensed clarity. The burden of perfection was lifted, replaced by a purpose. He realized that the essence of his craft wasn't technique but passion and commitment. This understanding became the guiding force as he began the final phase of his project, ready to blend modern designs with traditional structures in a way that honored his past and future.

Arun began to work again, but his approach was different. Instead of forcing the design, he let it flow naturally, allowing the traditional techniques to guide his modern ideas. The pressure to be perfect had lifted, replaced by a focus on authenticity and expression.

Without pausing his sanding, Arun greeted the familiar creak of the door with, "Late as usual, Bharat."

Bharat chuckled, shaking his head as he entered, dusting off his shirt. "Aai needed help with shopping. What can you do?"

Arun grinned, still focused on his work. "Well, you're here now. Take the sandpaper and begin sanding the edges of that base. We don't have much time before the unveiling."

He glanced at Bharat, who had just joined him in the workshop. "Mr. Prashant is organizing a significant exhibition, almost like an art fair," Arun said, his voice brimming with excitement and urgency. This is a chance for our work to be seen by everyone—critics, artists, and the entire community."This is a huge opportunity to showcase our work and get real feedback. We'll have to work hard, Bharat, to ensure everything is perfect."

Bharat picked up the sandpaper and moved to the other side of the table, his fingers running over the unfinished wood. "So, this is the famous project, huh? It looks... impressive. Different from your usual stuff."

Arun nodded, wiping sweat from his forehead. "Yeah, Prashant Chavan asked for something that blends tradition with modern elements. It's been challenging, but I think we're getting there."

Bharat worked in silence; the sound of sandpaper against wood filled the air. After a while, he glanced at Arun. "Do you think Appa will come to the unveiling?"

The question cast a shadow over them, hanging heavy in the air. Arun's hands stilled for a moment before he continued working. "I don't know," he replied quietly. "He hasn't said much since I told Aai about the project. But whether he comes or not... I have to do this."

Don't worry," Bharat said, giving Arun a reassuring pat on the shoulder. "He'll be there, even if he doesn't say a word. He's proud of you.

Arun smiled slightly, grateful for Bharat's support. "Thanks, Bharat. Let's focus on getting this done. There's still a lot of work ahead."

Bharat grinned and got back to sanding, his movements becoming more purposeful. "Don't worry. With both of us, we'll finish in time."

As they worked together, their combined skills created a familiar harmony. Bharat's steady hand and Arun's precise touch blended seamlessly. Their light-hearted banter dissolved the tension, offering a brief respite from the approaching deadline.

"You know," Bharat said after a while, his tone more serious, "whatever happens at the unveiling, this piece—it's yours. It's something new, something only you could've made. No one can take that away."

Arun looked up from his work, meeting Bharat's eyes. He felt a surge of gratitude for his friend's unwavering support. "I hope so, Bharat. I hope so."

Bharat nodded and returned to his task. "One hour," Arun affirmed. "Almost there." Bharat's gaze held the unfinished piece.

Dusk fell, the workshop lights flickering, yet they worked on.

Arun watched as the town gathered for the unveiling, a ripple of excitement spreading through the crowd, and his heart pounded in his chest. This was the culmination of all his struggles. Yet, amid the tension, peace washed over him. He had found his path—not to prove himself but to create, motivated by his artistic spirit. The challenges ahead remained, but Arun no longer felt lost. He was crafting something new while paying tribute to the legacy that had shaped him. Though reconciliation with his father was uncertain, this project had given him hope and belonging in his family's story.

The private viewing buzzed with anticipation, a low hum of conversation filling the air. Beside his sculpture—a testament to months of struggle, doubt, and unwavering determination—Arun felt his heart pound in his chest. But beneath the surface of excitement, a deeper turmoil brewed within him—would his parents attend the unveiling? Would they understand the choices he had made?

His mind drifted to the memory of his father's stern eyes and his mother's silent encouragement. Everything he had poured into his work was now laid bare. Would they see it as a tribute or a challenge? The apprehension of their disappointment tugged at him, darkening what should have been a moment of triumph.

Arun's gaze drifted to the entrance, hoping with each passing second that his parents would walk through the door and be here to witness this pivotal moment in his life. But what if they came and didn't understand? The fear constricted his chest—everything he'd worked for and valued, hanging in the balance.

While patrons and critics scrutinized his sculpture—a testament to months of struggle and unwavering dedication—Arun stood by, a mix of eagerness and apprehension churning within him. The piece, a striking fusion of modern and traditional elements, was the center of attention. Every murmur and thoughtful glance sent a jolt through him—was this his defining moment?

As patrons examined the piece, Arun's heart raced—each glance of whispered comments stirred the anxiety that had accompanied him throughout the creation process. Months of toil and doubt seemed to culminate in this moment, and he couldn't help but wonder—was it enough?" His thoughts drifted to his father. Would Ravji notice the homage in the base pattern—a subtle nod to the river where his craft was born? Or would he see only the deviation from tradition? The sculpture masterpiece, a stunning blend of modern design and traditional craftsmanship, was drawing attention. Every murmur and studied look heightened the suspense: would this be the work that changed everything?

In a quiet corner, Saarika, Sudhir, Prashant, and Arun discussed the artwork, their conversation a blend of thoughtful critique and easy laughter.

"It's finally out there," Arun thought, his mind flashing back to countless nights of hard work, each stroke filled with the fear of not living up to his father's legacy. But here, it was the culmination of his struggles standing tall in the middle of the room.

Saarika was the first to speak up, her eyes scanning the bullock cart with admiration and intrigue. "Arun, this cart is an exceptional piece of work. You've elegantly and innovatively combined traditional craftsmanship with contemporary design. The sleek lines and bold colors give it a modern flair, while the intricate carvings and inlaid patterns connect it deeply with our cultural roots. Collaborating with local artisans to include these regional motifs brings out the richness of our heritage."

Sudhir, examining the cart closely, added, "Absolutely brilliant. The removable cushions and footrests add comfort for long journeys, making it functional and user-friendly. The clever blending of ergonomic design with the traditional form preserves its aesthetic perfectly.

"And then there's the weatherproof canopy material—it's not just about aesthetics but also about making sure it performs well in different weather conditions."

Prashant, watching the conversation unfold, leaned in with a thoughtful smile. "I completely agree. This cart isn't just a combination of styles—it creates communication between eras. The custom carvings depicting the legend of King Vikramaditya and the wise sage Vetal add layers of narrative and artistic expression. The detailed scenes from their famous encounters, carved into the wood, breathe life into our folklore. Along with the inlaid brass and colored stones, these elements transform the cart into more than just a vehicle—a piece of living history, enhanced by modern touches. The weather protection ensures its enduring beauty and practicality.

Saarika continued, her excitement palpable. "And the built-in storage compartments! It's such a smart idea, Arun. You've transformed this cart from a simple vehicle into a versatile tool that answers a variety of needs. The hidden compartments keep the design clean but offer practical solutions for modern needs. It's a perfect example of innovation working alongside tradition."

Arun, feeling a mix of relief and nervousness, said, "Thank you all. My aim was to innovate within the framework of our tradition. Collaborating with artisans allowed me to keep the craftsmanship authentic while introducing elements like the removable sections for custom carvings. My goal was to demonstrate how innovation can enrich tradition.

Prashant's expression turned serious but encouraging. "You've achieved that beautifully. This cart symbolizes how tradition and modernity can coexist. I understand your concerns about your father's reaction, though. It's a significant departure from what he's accustomed to, but also a bold step forward. Your work could inspire new interpretations of our craft."

Sudhir added, "This cart beautifully blends the old and the new, marking a new phase in our artistic development. The sustainable materials reflect both modern concerns and our deep connection to the earth. These innovative processes enhance our traditions. I'm confident that even Ravji will recognize its worth eventually."

Despite the praise, Arun's thoughts lingered on his father, wondering if Ravji would see the cart's innovations as honoring tradition or straying too far from their roots.

As Arun's mind clouded with worry, a familiar hand rested on his shoulder. He turned to see Bharat, his face a mix of pride and concern. Bharat seemed to sense the turmoil beneath Arun's calm exterior.

"Arun," Bharat said warmly, "you've done something incredible here. But I know you're worried about what your father will think."

Arun sighed. "I am. I wonder if he'll see this as straying from tradition or appreciate how I've tried to honor it."

Bharat nodded. "Your father respects the craft. I believe he'll recognize the skill and courage it took to create something new."

Arun found comfort in Bharat's words. "I hope so. I want him to be proud of what I've accomplished."

"He will be," Bharat reassured him. "Remember, you didn't just create this for him—you did it for yourself. That's what matters most."

Arun felt a wave of gratitude. "Thank you, Bharat. Your support means everything."

"You're not alone," Bharat smiled. "No matter what happens, you've already succeeded by staying true to yourself."

Saarika turned to Sudhir, a curious expression on her face. "What strikes you most about it, Sudhir? You seem deep in thought."

Sudhir, his gaze softening, replied, "Arun has masterfully integrated traditional techniques into a modern design, retaining the essence of both. It's as if he's speaking two languages fluently—honoring the past while conversing with the present. It's a testament to his skill and vision."

Prashant chimed in, "That's exactly what makes this piece special. It's not just about aesthetics; it's about creating a dialogue between different eras of craftsmanship. Arun has created a bridge that few dare to walk across. He's achieved that brilliantly."

Saarika nodded, her eyes still reflecting admiration. "And it's not just about the technical aspects. There's an emotional depth to this piece. You can see the journey in every curve and line the internal battle between loyalty to tradition and the urge to innovate. Arun's struggles are reflected in it."

Saarika's words washed over him, and a warm pride surged through Arun, spreading from his chest to his fingertips. He had poured his heart into every detail of the piece, reflecting his hopes and fears. "I've poured a lot of myself into this project. It's been a challenging but rewarding process."

Sudhir's gaze turned to Prashant. "You've taken quite a gamble with this commission, Prashant. But it seems to have paid off. Do you think this will influence how people view the blending of tradition and modernity in art?"

Prashant smiled, his eyes twinkling. "I believe it will. This piece has the potential to start conversations and challenge perceptions. Art should provoke thought, and this does just that. It's a bold move, but one that I think will resonate with many."

Prashant placed a reassuring hand on Arun's shoulder. "You've not only succeeded, Arun; you've excelled. You've shown that innovation and tradition don't have to be mutually exclusive. You've bridged the gap between the past and the future, something few can claim to have done."

Saarika added, "And that's something worth celebrating. This piece has a place in the future of art, but it also pays homage to the past. It's a conversation between what was and what could be—a remarkable achievement."

Arun's gaze shifted to a corner of the room where a framed photograph of his parents hung. The picture showed Ravji and Vatsala, their faces reflecting pride and love. His throat tightened as memories of their guidance and expectations flooded his mind. Arun's thoughts turned to them, and he spoke softly, though clearly enough for his companions to hear.

Saarika's expression softened. "They've given you roots, Arun, and you've spread your wings. Your parents must be proud of you, and it's evident in your work—in the craftsmanship and the heart you've put into it."

Tears welling in his eyes, Arun looked at Saarika, Sudhir, and Prashant, their faces filled with support. "Thank you," he said, his voice thick with emotion. "Sharing this with you all has meant everything."

The evening unfolded in a spirit of celebration, the earlier tension dissolving into laughter and easy conversation. Arun felt a deep sense of satisfaction, knowing his work had touched those present and paid homage to his roots. While the future remained unwritten, the warmth and recognition he received offered a beacon of hope.

A week had passed since the unveiling, and the silence from his parents gnawed at Arun. Early morning sunlight didn't reach his restless heart. At his bench, he carved with precision, each cut a heavy, unanswered question. The success of his project had sparked new ideas, but they couldn't quiet the void. Every stroke of the carving seemed more like a plea, his mind wandering back to the one approval he craved most—his father's. The stillness was suffocating as if waiting for a word that never came.

Every stroke of the carving seemed more like a plea, his mind wandering back to the one approval he craved most—his father's. The stillness was suffocating as if waiting for a word that never came. Just then, the door creaked open, and Bharat entered with a broad smile, a local newspaper tucked under one arm, and a crisp white envelope in hand. Arun looked up, wiping his hands on his apron.

"Good morning, Arun! You'll want to see this," Bharat said, placing the newspaper on the bench.

Arun's eyes flicked to the headline, which prominently featured his name. "Local Artisan Breaks Boundaries: Arun's Work Gains National Attention," it read. His eyes widened as he read the article, each word a testament to his success, the praise from art critics and patrons washing over him.

But as he read the praise, a pang of unease gnawed at him—what good was national attention if the one person whose approval he craved remained distant?

But it was the envelope in Bharat's hand that intrigued him more.

"And this," Bharat continued, holding out the envelope with a mischievous grin, "is something special."

Arun took the envelope, noting the elegant script that spelt his name. He opened it carefully, revealing a letter inside. His eyes widened as he read the contents.

"It's an invitation," Arun murmured, almost in disbelief. "To an exhibition in Mumbai. They want me to showcase my work."

Bharat clapped him on the shoulder. "This is it, Arun! Your big break. "This exhibition offers a national stage for you and our town."

As they chatted, Arun's mind drifted to thoughts of his parents. The newspaper article and the invitation were achievements he had long dreamed of, but they felt incomplete without his father's acknowledgment. His mother, Vatsala, had always been his silent supporter, nurturing his creativity in the shadows of tradition. But it was Ravji's forgiveness and acceptance that Arun yearned for the most. No amount of acclaim could fill the void left by the rift between them. As he worked, Arun couldn't help but wonder if his parents would come to see his work in Mumbai. Would this finally earn his father's acceptance, or would he face continued rejection, rooted in tradition? The thought gnawed at him, making each pass of the sandpaper feel more laborious as if he were smoothing his anxieties into the wood's surface. He imagined the unveiling—crowds gathered, eyes full of admiration, yet the one pair of eyes he longed to meet might not even be there. The possibility of his father's absence brought a tinge of sadness, reminding him that true success meant more than just external validation.

"I can see the worry in your eyes, Arun," Bharat began gently, his voice carrying the weight of their long friendship. "I know this is a big moment that you worked so hard for. But I also know you're still hoping for your father's approval, aren't you?" Arun's eyes flickered. with a mix of surprise and resignation, acknowledging the truth in Bharat's words.

Bharat continued his voice soft and understanding, "Just remember, you've already achieved something incredible. You've pushed boundaries, inspired others, and stayed true to yourself. That's something to be proud of, even if it takes time for others to see it."

Arun nodded slowly, feeling the weight of his anxiety ease slightly. Bharat's words were a balm, offering comfort amid his uncertainty.

Arun smiled, the weight of the moment settling in. "Arun smiled faintly. "I hope you're right, Bharat. I want my work to bridge the past and the future."

They were interrupted by the arrival of a few other artisans from the town. Ganpat, Fakira, and Damodar had come to visit, each curious about the buzz surrounding Arun's latest achievements.

"We heard the news," Fakira said, his eyes twinkling with pride. "You've done well, Arun. Very well."

Ganpat nodded in agreement. "You're making us all look at things differently, boy. It's good for the community. Keeps us growing."

Damodar, ever the traditionalist, gave a gruff nod. "I wasn't sure at first, but I can see the value in what you're doing. It's important to keep the old ways alive, but maybe there's room for something new as well."

As the older men spoke, gratitude swelled within Arun, yet a familiar ache lingered beneath it, longing for his father's voice to offer the words of approval he so deeply craved. Their praise meant more to him than they knew, but it wasn't enough to quiet the ache in his heart. "Thank you," he said quietly. "It means a lot to hear that from you."

While the older artisans discussed the community's changes, Arun's thoughts returned to Ravji. Unbeknownst to him, his father had been quietly following his success, the town's proud whispers reaching his ears. But this pride was tinged with regret—regret for the growing distance between them and the unspoken words.

The rhythmic scrape of steel on stone echoed in Ravji's workshop as he meticulously sharpened his chisel. The familiar scents of wood and varnish offered little comfort as his thoughts turned to Arun's success. Each deliberate stroke carried the weight of unspoken words, a heavy burden of regret. Had his silence been interpreted as disapproval? Pride had prevented him from expressing his admiration, and now a vast gulf separated them.

As the sun dipped below the horizon, Ravji paused, his heart heavy. Arun's work, a seamless blend of tradition and innovation, stirred something deep within him—a quiet pride, reluctantly acknowledged. Though the words remained unspoken, a shift occurred. For the first time, Ravji saw his son's courage in forging his path. Tradition and innovation, father and son—slowly, a bridge was being built.

The Mumbai invitation rested on his workbench, a tangible promise of the journey to come. It wasn't merely an opportunity; it was a confirmation of his chosen path. With his friends' support, his community's inspiration, and his father's silent watch, Arun felt prepared to move forward.

Arun's hands moved mechanically, the chisel biting into the wood with every stroke. Yet his mind was elsewhere, caught in doubt and longing. The upcoming exhibition loomed, not just as a test of his craft but of something far deeper. Would his success mend the distance between him and his father or widen it further?

Each cut into the wood was a struggle against the weight of unspoken words, a tangible attempt to erase years of silent disapproval. Arun's heart pounded his mind a whirlwind of thoughts. Though uncertainty clouded his focus, a decision began to solidify beneath the anxiety. His hands trembled as he paused, his gaze fixed on the nearly finished piece. It was more than art—it was a bridge, a desperate plea for connection. Pride and fear had held him back for too long. The moment for action had arrived.

With a sharp exhale, Arun laid down the chisel. He would face them, not as a son seeking validation but as a man ready to reconcile with his past. His heart pounded with a newfound resolve; the time had come to shatter the silence that had defined their relationship.

He would face his parents, not for redemption alone, but to finally heal the rift that had kept them apart.

CHAPTER SIX

A Legacy Renewed

He could still hear the echoes of their last argument, the harsh words exchanged before he left home to pursue his dreams. Ravji's voice, usually calm and patient, had cracked with frustration: "You're throwing away everything our ancestors built, Arun. Tradition is not something to be discarded!" Arun had retorted, "But Appa, we can't cling to the past forever! We need to evolve!" Memories crashed over Arun as he neared his family's house—his father's hands, calloused yet gentle, teaching him to carve. The world was simpler than his father, a role model. But the urge to innovate had driven them apart.

As he approached his home, Arun's heart was heavy with uncertainty. Each step felt like it carried the weight of the past, and the memories of their last argument echoed in his mind, louder with each passing moment. He couldn't help but wonder—would his father ever truly understand his choices? Would this be the moment they could finally reconcile, or would it push them further apart? The questions gnawed at him, making each footfall feel heavier.

He could still hear the echoes of their last argument, the harsh words exchanged before he left home to pursue his dreams. Ravji's voice, usually calm and patient, had cracked with frustration: "You're throwing away everything our ancestors built, Arun. Tradition is not something to be discarded!" Arun countered, his voice sharp with conviction, "But Appa, we can't cling to the past forever! We need to evolve!"

Now, standing at the threshold of his home, those memories weigh heavily on him. His steps faltered as doubt crept in—what if it was too late to mend what was broken? Vatsala, his mother, was the first to greet him. Her face, lined with years of worry and love, softened into a warm smile as she saw him.

"Arun," Vatsala said, her voice trembling with emotion. "You're home."

"Aai," Arun began, his voice trembling as emotion surged within him. "I want to apologise, Appa. I want him back." He paused, swallowing the knot in his throat. "I think about you both all the time—every day, every moment I'm away. I can't forget the love and memories we used to have. But with Appa, it's different. It hurts, Aai. It hurts me the way things are now between us. I feel offended by the regret, which I am unable to overcome. I've spent so much time trying to find my way, but I can't stop thinking about him—about how distant we've become. I need to fix it before it's too late. I can't keep living like this. Help me to escape this agony, Aai, please."

Vatsala had been the silent witness to the growing distance between her husband and son. Her heart had broken a little more each day they were apart, and now, seeing them come together, she felt an overwhelming sense of relief. She had always believed that love would bring them back together, and her faith was rewarded in this moment. Vatsala's eyes filled with tears as she embraced him. "We've missed you so much. Your father... he's been struggling with your absence. I've been hoping you'd come back to us."

As she held him, Arun was transported back to the time when he had fallen ill as a child. He remembered how his mother had stayed up all night, her cool hands soothing his fevered brow. She had always been the anchor in his life; her quiet strength and unconditional love were a constant source of comfort.

Vatsala nodded, her gaze filled with a mixture of sorrow and hope. "He's in the workshop. He's been waiting for you, even if he never said so. Let's go."

Together, they walked to the workshop. The scent of wood and varnish hit Arun first, a wave of memories washing over him. He remembered his first visit, the smell of fresh shavings, and his father's pride as he explained the craft. That pride had been both a blessing and a curse, driving them apart as Arun sought to innovate.

Vatsala pushed open the old wooden door, which creaked in protest. The sight of Ravji bent over his workbench was familiar and foreign. The workshop, once a place of discord, now seemed to hold the promise of reconciliation.

"Appa," Arun said softly, stepping inside. Ravji looked up, his expression a mix of surprise and wariness.

Ravji slowly set down his tools, his eyes widening in surprise as he met Arun's gaze. The weight of years between them was palpable in his voice. "Arun... you're here? What brings you here after all this time?"

Arun felt a lump form in his throat, his heart heavy with unspoken words. His mind raced, searching for the right words to bridge the chasm that had grown between them. He took a deep breath, trying to steady himself. "I'm back, Appa," Arun said, his voice trembling with emotion. "I can't go on like this—I want us to find our way back to each other."

Ravji's brows furrowed slightly, his tone gruff but tinged with curiosity. "Find our way? After all this time, now you think of this?"

As Ravji listened to Arun's words, the memories of their arguments clashed with the pride he secretly felt for his son's accomplishments. He wanted to hold onto his anger to protect the traditions that had defined him. But with each word Arun spoke, Ravji felt the walls he had built around his heart begin to crumble. His pride had become a crushing burden.

"Appa," Arun began, his voice trembling, "I know I've hurt you. I know I disregarded your advice and went against everything you taught me. But it wasn't disrespectful. It was fear... fear that I could never be the man you are."

Ravji's expression softened, the harsh lines of his face easing into something more vulnerable. He remembered the day Arun had left—how he had watched from the doorway, too proud to call him back, too angry to admit his fear of losing his son to a world he didn't understand.

"You always had your way, Arun," Ravji said quietly. He paused, his gaze dropping to the floor as if searching for the right words. "I just couldn't see past my expectations to understand it. I thought you were throwing away everything I worked for, everything our family stood for."

Arun shook his head, his eyes brimming with tears. "I was wrong to leave the way I did, to distance myself from you and Aai. But every step I took, every piece I created, I did with you in mind. Even when I was lost, I wanted to make you proud. I wanted to prove that I wasn't abandoning our heritage—I was trying to find a way to carry it forward."

Ravji's eyes glistened as he listened, the unspoken tension between father and son beginning to dissolve. He remembered the pride he felt the first time he saw Arun's work in a magazine—how his heart had swelled with pride and pain, knowing that his son had succeeded but feeling the sting of their estrangement.

Ravji couldn't deny the skill and vision in Arun's designs. He recognised the courage it took to forge a new path, even if he'd never admitted it. For the first time, he allowed himself to feel pride in his son.

"I watched you from afar, Arun. I saw your work and I was proud. but I couldn't bring myself to say it. I was too stubborn, too afraid to admit that maybe... maybe you were right in your way."

Arun stepped closer, his voice trembling with sincerity. He could see the conflict in his father's eyes—the battle between pride and the deep love that had never faded. "Appa, I don't want to be right or wrong. I want to be your son again. I want us to work together to create something that honours our legacies. It feels incomplete without your blessing."

Ravji's stern expression finally broke, his shoulders sagging as if releasing years of unspoken tension. A tear slipped down his cheek as he reached to grasp Arun's shoulder. "You never stopped being my son, Arun. I was the one who pushed you away, blinded by my pride. If you're willing... I'd be honoured to create something that will represent us—our family, traditions, and future."

Arun's tears flowed freely now as he embraced his father, the years of distance and misunderstanding melting away in that moment. The warmth of the embrace was unlike anything Arun had felt in years—a reassurance that he was finally home. "Appa," Arun whispered, his voice choked with emotion, "I've made many mistakes, and I hurt you. I'm so sorry for that. But I've always carried your teachings with me. even when I seemed to be going in a different direction. Your approval means everything to me."

Ravji, his eyes glistening with unshed tears, placed a hand on Arun's shoulder, his grip firm but gentle. "Arun, my son... It was never about needing your forgiveness. I only wanted you to find your path, even if I didn't understand it initially. Seeing the man you've become, I realise now that you've honoured our legacy in your way."

Arun leaned back slightly, his gaze locking with his father's. His voice was soft, yet brimming with profound respect. "Appa, I'm so proud to be your son. Everything I've accomplished, I owe to you and Aai—to the values you've instilled in me. My success feels hollow without your acceptance, Appa. I need your blessing to feel like I've truly arrived."

Ravji embraced Arun tightly; the bond between father and son rekindled in that heartfelt moment. "You've always had my blessing, Arun. I'm proud of you, more than words can express. Let's build something together that shows the world who we are."

Vatsala, quietly standing by, wiped her eyes and smiled through her tears. "This is the moment I've prayed for for so long. Let's make something beautiful together." The weight of the years lifted from her shoulders, and in that moment, she felt the joy of seeing her family whole again; their hearts healed.

Vatsala sensed it was time to bring some warmth back into the room. She approached Ravji placed her hand on his arm and said gently, "Let's set the work aside for now. Don't you think it's been a while since we all sat down together? Let's grab some tea, settle in, and share those moments that still make us smile. Remember that time? Maybe we'll even laugh like we used to—the sound of clinking cups, the surprise in our eyes as old memories come rushing back. Meanwhile, I'll prepare a meal with all your favourite dishes—and, of course, some sweets—to celebrate this reunion."

Ravji happily nodded, understanding the importance of Vatsala's suggestion. A wave of relief washed over him, and he was grateful for his mother's ability to nurture this fragile moment of reconciliation. He looked at his mother with gratitude, recognising her wisdom in creating this much-needed space for healing.

Vatsala smiled warmly and headed to the kitchen, leaving Ravji and Arun to sit and begin reminiscing. As she busied herself with cooking, the familiar sounds and smells of home filled the air, transforming the house into a sanctuary of comfort and love. The clattering of utensils and the aroma of spices became a comforting backdrop to the conversation, slowly unravelling years of distance and misunderstandings between father and son.

The sun dipped low, casting long shadows across Ravji's workshop as father and son stood side by side, chisels in hand. Weeks had passed since their reconciliation, and now they worked with a quiet rhythm—two generations, one purpose. The chariot, a long-pending project of Ravji's, had become their shared vision. It was no longer just a symbol of tradition but a testament to the merging of past and present, of two minds working in harmony.

Arun ran his hand along the smooth, intricately carved wood, feeling his father's craft and his innovations meld seamlessly—a legacy of craftsmanship, generations in the making. Yet, new touches—Arun's touches—dotted the structure, subtle yet significant, bridging two worlds. With the festival just around the corner, the pressure to complete the chariot is mounted. The once-unfinished project, gathering dust, would become their offering to the town temple—a gift of tradition and innovation, a symbol of unity gracing the temple grounds as part of the grand decoration.

The unveiling day arrived swiftly. Excitement hummed through the town square as people shuffled closer, exchanging eager whispers. Children darted between the adults, and elders craned their necks, all eyes fixed on the stage where the reveal was about to unfold. Ravji and Arun stood before the covered chariot, its embroidered cloth hiding weeks of labour, reconciliation, and understanding.

A hush fell over the crowd as Shripat, the town head, stepped forward, his turban gleaming white in the evening light. "Today," he announced, his voice strong and steady, "we witness the meeting of tradition and innovation. This creation, born of both, is a gift from Ravji and Arun to our town and temple."

Arun's pulse quickened as he looked at the gathered town—elders who had once scorned his modern ideas and younger faces eager to see something new. He caught his mother's eye; Vatsala stood proudly at the front, her quiet strength palpable.

As the crowd gathered, all eyes turned toward the town head, an elderly man in a white turban, his walking stick tapping softly as he approached the chariot. Ravji and Arun shared a significant glance.

With a polite nod from Ravji, Shripat moved to stand beside the covered chariot. "Today, we honour not only our traditions but the spirit of innovation that carries them forward," Shripat announced, his voice steady and commanding. His weathered hand grasped the edge of the cloth, and with a slow, deliberate motion, he pulled it away.

The embroidered cloth fell, revealing the chariot—a breathtaking sight. Traditional carvings of deities and intricate floral patterns adorned the base. Above, sleek, flowing curves ascended, lending the structure a sense of movement and grace. The modern touches blended seamlessly with the age-old craftsmanship, creating a vision of tradition and tomorrow.

A wave of awe washed over the crowd as the chariot's beauty was unveiled. Whispers of admiration and astonishment rippled through the square as the town witnessed the perfect fusion of past and present, tradition and innovation.

Ganpat, a respected elder, approached first, examining the chariot with narrow eyes. "Ravji," he began, running his hand over the base of the chariot, "this woodwork is as fine as anything you've ever done, but there's something different here." His fingers traced a flowing pattern carved into the side, and the grooves were more fluid and dynamic than the usual geometric designs. "These curves... this is not the work of our tradition. What have you done?"

Ravji smiled, nodding toward Arun. "You're right, Ganpat. The base is carved in the traditional style—straight, angular patterns like we've always done. Arun introduced a new technique. He suggested using finer tools to create these flowing, organic shapes. It's a way of capturing movement, something we've never done before in our chariots."

Fakira, another elder known for his staunch defense of tradition, frowned slightly but leaned in for a closer look. "But does it hold the same meaning? Our designs are symbolic—the straight lines and angles represent order, the balance of life. What do these curves represent?"

Arun stepped forward, eager to explain. "Fakira Baba, the curves represent fluidity and growth—how life doesn't always move in straight lines. It reflects our world today—tradition and progress coexist. But it doesn't replace the old symbolism. Look closely at the base of the chariot; the traditional designs are still there, supporting the entire structure. The curves flow upwards from them, showing that innovation can grow out of tradition without losing its roots."

Damodar, a fellow craftsman, squatted down to inspect the intricate wheels of the chariot. "These wheels... they're amazing. Normally, we carve spokes in a rigid, symmetrical pattern. But here, the spokes seem to twist, almost like they're spiralling outward. How did you manage this, Arun?"

Arun smiled, proud of the innovation. "The wheels were one of the most challenging parts. I wanted them to look like they were in motion, even when still. Instead of the usual straight spokes, I used twist carving, which gives the illusion of movement. It's something

I picked up during my time abroad. The challenge was keeping the wheel structurally sound while creating the twist. But we figured out a way by combining traditional joinery with a modern design."

Damodar nodded, impressed. "Clever design. The wheels look alive, almost ready to take off, yet sturdy, rooted in our traditional construction."

Once sceptical of innovation and protective of tradition, Sudhir now undeniably appreciated Arun's talent for blending old and new.

Unable to contain his excitement, Sudhir stepped forward, eyes gleaming as he admired the chariot. "Look at the canopy!" he exclaimed, pointing to the top. "That's not the usual flat design we've always used for the temple chariots. It resembles the temple dome itself, with its layered, intricate details. Arun, how did you manage to carve something so unique?"

Ravji's smile radiated pride for Arun. "Traditionally, we kept it flat and simple, focusing on the carvings below. But Arun envisioned something grander, reflecting the temple's majesty. So, we layered it like a pagoda, adding intricate carvings of deities and symbols. The journey was longer than expected, but the destination is breathtaking."

Ganpat, studying the design, folded his arms thoughtfully. "This is impressive. But I'm concerned about the structural integrity. Do these new curves and twists compromise its sturdiness?"

Arun answered this time, confident in their solution. "We had the same concern, Ganpat Kaka. That's why we didn't just jump into it. We kept the main frame of the chariot exactly as it's always been—using the same wood and traditional joinery techniques. The innovations we added are all on top of that solid foundation. The base, wheels, and frame are all built traditionally to ensure the chariot remains strong. The modern elements are enhancements, not replacements."

Fakira, quietly absorbing the conversation, spoke up again. "I see. So, the foundation is still ours—our tradition, our methods. And the new designs are... adornments?"

Arun nodded. "Exactly. Think of it as evolution, not replacement. The chariot still stands on the same foundation but reaches toward the future, just like we do."

Damodar, running his hand along the chariot's surface again, smiled. "I must admit, I was sceptical about these changes. But seeing it now... it's a beautiful marriage of tradition and innovation. It respects our traditions while showing that we're not afraid to move forward."

Sudhir, inspired, added, "This chariot is a call to action. We must all find ways to honour our traditions while embracing progress. The past is important, but so is the future. Let this chariot be our guide."

Ravji, voice steady with newfound wisdom, said, "That's what Arun taught me. For years, I resisted change, thinking it would destroy everything we built. But now I see that innovation can support tradition, just like these modern designs support the structure of the chariot. We don't have to choose between the two—we can have both."

Ganpat, finally convinced, smiled broadly. "This chariot will be the pride of our town when it's displayed at the festival. It's a testament to who we are—honouring our past while embracing the future."

As the town gathered around the chariot, admiring its craftsmanship, Shripat, deeply moved, stepped forward. "This chariot symbolises more than just tradition—it reflects a journey of growth, unity, and innovation. Arun, would you share a few words with us?"

Arun hesitated, emotions swirling within him, before stepping forward. "This chariot isn't just a creation—it's a reflection of everything my father and I have gone through," he began, his voice steady but filled with emotion. "I couldn't have done it without the support of so many. My mother, Aai, was our strength through everything. Bharat, my friend, always believed in me when I had doubts. Fakira Kaka's wisdom guided me back to my roots, and Savitri Kaki's encouragement kept me moving forward."

He paused, glancing at his father with a soft smile. "This chariot is our way of honouring tradition while embracing innovation. It's a mark of respect for our past and hope for our future. Thank you, everyone, for being part of this journey."

Bathed in the golden light, father and son stood side by side, united not only by the chariot but by a shared vision that bridged generations.

The late afternoon sun cast a golden glow over the town, its warm rays filtering through the Neem tree under which Ravji, Vatsala, and Arun sat. Outside the familiar walls of the workshop, the three shared a peaceful moment, the tension that once thickened the air between father and son now dissipating like the soft breeze that rustled the leaves. Vatsala quietly refilled their plates, her gentle smile reflecting the quiet joy of a mother seeing her family together again. Arun leaned back, letting the sunlight wash over him. For the first time in years, he felt free from the weight of unspoken expectations.

Bharat and Savitri arrived all smiles. "Arun!" Bharat called out, bursting with pride. "The whole town is buzzing about your chariot!"

Savitri added, "And guess what? The newspaper wants to feature it!"

Arun's heart swelled with a mix of disbelief and happiness. He stood to greet his old friend and Savitri Kaki, a smile spreading across his face. "Really?" he asked, his voice full of wonder.

Savitri, eyes twinkling, nodded in agreement. "You've shown everyone that honouring tradition doesn't mean turning away from the future. You and Ravji have given the town something that connects generations."

Ravji, silent but observant, exchanged a glance with Arun. Ravji's eyes widened in surprise, his gaze locking onto Arun, a mix of shock and quiet pride evident in his expression. No words passed between them, but the connection was unmistakable—stronger than before, a bond that had once frayed now mending in the shared silence.

As they talked, the faint tapping of a stick announced Fakira's arrival. His familiar presence carried the quiet wisdom he always possessed. His steps were slow but steady, yet his eyes were sharp and twinkling. Arun and Ravji instinctively rose, exchanging a glance before turning to greet him. Fakira, the old craftsman, faced a map of wisdom and stepped into view, commanding respect. Father and son greeted him with folded hands and bow heads, acknowledging the quiet authority he held.

"Fakira baba," Arun said warmly, his voice filled with reverence.

Ravji, standing beside his son, added, "It's an honour to have you here, kaka."

"Namaste, Fakira Kaka," Vatsala greeted him warmly, rising to offer him a seat beside them.

Fakira smiled, his twinkling eyes acknowledging their respect with a quiet nod as he settled onto a stool. He gazed at Ravji and Arun, his voice heavy with the wisdom of generations. "The future of our craft is in good hands," he said, words echoing the wisdom passed down through generations.

The group fell silent, the air filled with the quiet hum of the town winding down for the evening. Fakira's gaze moved between father and son. "This journey you're on... I've seen it before. Your father and I faced the same struggle, Ravji. Balancing what was and what could be—it's never a simple path."

Ravji nodded, his eyes lowering in thought. "I never imagined I'd be the one resisting change," he murmured.

Fakira leaned forward, his tone softening. "Change is difficult, but it's what keeps our craft alive. You've guided Arun well, but you've also allowed him to find his way. The hardest part of being a father—knowing when to let go."

Bharat's voice cut in, brimming with pride. "You should've seen the chariot, Fakira Kaka. Arun's work feels fresh, but it fits—it feels like it's always been part of our tradition."

Fakira nodded again, his gaze landing on Arun. "I don't doubt it for a second. Arun, you've managed to capture something special. You've taken what's been passed down to you and given it new life.

That's what makes your work important."

Vatsala, ever the gentle host, poured tea for everyone. Her smile brightened the already warm atmosphere. "This moment wouldn't be complete without you, Fakira Kaka," she said.

Fakira's eyes softened as he looked at her. "Vatsala Beti, you've always known how to bring us all together," he replied, his voice touched with affection.

The sun dipped lower, casting long shadows, as the group sat in quiet reflection. The scent of tea mingled with the sounds of the town, creating a moment of peace. Fakira's presence, like the golden light of the setting sun, seemed to bridge the past and the present.

As they sipped their tea, Fakira spoke once more. "There's a verse from the Bhagavad Gita I've been thinking about," he said, his eyes sparkling with wisdom. He paused, letting the anticipation build before reciting it, the words carrying the depth of their shared journey.

Ravji and Arun exchanged another glance, a silent understanding passing between them. Fakira's words, like the evening sun, settled deep in their hearts, marking this moment as one they would carry with them forever.

श्रेयान्स्वधर्मो वगिुण: परधर्मात्स्वनुष्ठतिात्
स्वधर्मे नधिनं श्रेय: परधर्मो भयावह: ॥

Arun listened intently as Fakira recited the Sanskrit verse, the words resonating deep within him. Fakira translated the verse, his voice calm and steady:

"It is better to perform one's duty imperfectly than to perform another's perfectly.

One's duty performed imperfectly is preferable to another's performed perfectly, as performing one's is safer and preferable, whereas performing another's can be fraught with danger."

The words lingered in the air, thick and resonant, each syllable weighted with the gravity of a life fully lived. Fakira wasn't just offering advice; he was revealing the hard-won truths that had shaped his own life. The verse was more than a guide—it was a mirror, reflecting the rugged paths they had chosen, strewn with light and shadow. It whispered to them of resilience, of the unyielding spirit required to tread such roads. At that moment, the verse became a testament to their journey, a quiet affirmation that every stumble, every scar, and every hard-won triumph belonged to them alone. It was a call to own their imperfect choices and walk forward, their lives firmly in their hands.

Ravji's eyes softened, a mixture of surprise and understanding flickering. He nodded slowly, the weight of years spent clinging to tradition easing as a quiet pride for Arun began to take hold. Though he said nothing, the tension in his posture melted, revealing a man finally ready to accept his son's chosen path.

The truth of Fakira's words resonated deeply with Arun. He had wrestled with the conflict between duty and his heart's true calling. Now, he saw clearly: his imperfect journey had been essential to discovering his true self. The verse, spoken by Fakira, perfectly encapsulated this journey of both craft and spirit.

"You have both come a long way," Fakira said, his gaze shifting between Ravji and Arun. "Ravji, you held onto the traditions, preserving them with all your might. And Arun, you chose to carve your path, even when it meant straying from the family's traditions. But now, look at what you've created together. It is not a compromise; it is a new legacy. This workshop, this piece you're working on, is a testament to the truth that the Bhagavad Gita teaches us: to honour one's path, to embrace one's duty, even when it leads into unknown territory."

Ravji nodded slowly, the weight of Fakira's words sinking in. "It was difficult," he admitted, his voice soft. "I couldn't see beyond my expectations, my fear of losing what my father had built. But Arun... he showed me that tradition isn't about holding onto the past; it's about carrying its spirit into the future."

Arun's eyes met his father's, and for the first time, he saw not just the stern craftsman but a man who had learnt to let go, accept, and grow.

"Appa," Arun said, his voice filled with gratitude, "I couldn't have done this without you. Your teachings are in everything I create, even the pieces that seem different. My path, though imperfect, is mine, and it honours everything you've taught me. This workshop, this legacy—it belongs to both of us. I want to keep building it with you."

Fakira smiled, a lightness filling his heart. "That is the essence of the Gita's wisdom, Arun. Each of us has a path, a duty that is uniquely ours. It may not always be perfect, but it is true. And when we embrace it, we find our true selves—and our true connection to those who came before us. This legacy you both are creating is living proof of that truth."

As Fakira prepared to leave, he paused, turning to the two men who had become like family. His voice, usually so steady, held a note of emotion impossible to miss. "Remember," he said, his eyes misting slightly, "the greatest legacy is not in the works we leave behind, but in the love and understanding we pass on. Your bond, your shared vision—the true inheritance you will give to the next generation."

He placed a hand on Arun's shoulder. "Remember, the path is yours, but it carries the strength of those before you. Honour it, and you'll never lose your way. And Ravji," he added, turning to the respected craftsman, "you've done well to allow your son the space to find his way. You've created something timeless, blending the old with the new."

Vatsala, silently watching, stepped forward, her eyes glistening with unshed tears, her voice trembling slightly. "Fakira Kaka, your words have always been a guiding light for us. I see how they've shaped this family, this workshop, and this moment. The love and understanding you speak of—they are what bind us together."

Arun nodded, his heart full. "Thank you, Fakira Ji. Your words mean more than I can say."

Fakira smiled and a twinkle in his eyes. "Then let your actions speak for you, Arun. Create a legacy that tells your story and your father's for generations. And remember, the greatest legacy is not just in the works you leave behind, but in the hearts you touch along the way."

As Fakira left the workshop, the group lingered, savouring the warmth. Outside, the town settled into the calm of evening, but inside that humble space, a fire had been lit—a fire that would continue to burn brightly in the hearts of Ravji, Arun, and all those touched by their journey.

Their legacy lay not in the tools, but in the bonds they forged, the love they nurtured, and the future they embraced together.